WADSWORTH PHILOSOPHERS SERIES

ON

LEIBNIZ

Garrett Thomson
College of Wooster

WADSWORTH

THOMSON LEARNING

Australia • Canada • Mexico • Singapore • Spain
United Kingdom • United States

Printed in the United States of America
1 2 3 4 5 6 7 04 03 02 01 00

For permission to use material from this text, contact us:
Web: http://www.thomsonrights.com
Fax: 1-800-730-2215
Phone: 1-800-730-2214

For more information, contact:
Wadsworth/Thomson Learning, Inc.
10 Davis Drive
Belmont, CA 94002-3098
USA
http://www.wadsworth.com

ISBN: 0-534-57634-6

CONTENTS

Preface

> When I err in my opinions of persons, I prefer to err on the side of charity. And it is the same with respect to their writings. I endeavor to find in them not what may be blamed, but what may be praised and that from which I may learn something (Mackie, p. 277).

Leibniz was the most brilliant intellect of the seventeenth century. He was probably the most knowledgeable person of the period, too. He felt a deep obligation to understand as much of the universe as he could. He thought that this was the best way for him to benefit humanity. He studied tirelessly and managed to cram the work of several lifetimes into one. His approach to philosophy, as the above quotation indicates, was very open and synthetic. He combined the major philosophical currents from his time and antiquity into a new whole. Moreover, he was more than a philosopher. He was a mathematician, diplomat, inventor, lawyer, librarian, and more besides, and his experience in these other professions informs his philosophy. As a result of all these factors, Leibniz's philosophy is quite extraordinary. It is very broad in scope, but also some of his conclusions are quite startling. In this book, I will try to show the breadth of Leibniz's thought, and make his conclusions plain by revealing the reasoning that leads to them.

I would like to thank Prof. Dan Kolak and my mother, June Thomson, for their comments on this manuscript. I dedicate this work with love to my son, Andrew.

1

1
A Thousand and One Distractions

Gottfried Wilhelm Leibniz was a person of action as well as a scholar. A professional diplomat, a mining engineer, and an inventor, he also worked as a royal historian and librarian. As an academic, he was a world famous philosopher and mathematician, as well as being a trained lawyer. His accomplishments in some of these fields is outstanding. Together they amount to an extraordinarily active life. One edition of the works of Leibniz, contained in six volumes, testify to the wide scope of his interests:

Theology
Philosophy including his work in the sciences
Mathematics
Chinese history and philosophy
Diplomatic works
Treatises in philology and etymology

This is by no means the complete writings of Leibniz, which is still being edited, and of which 20 volumes have been published.

The enormous breadth of his work can be traced back to his early childhood. His father, who was a professor of philosophy at Leipzig, died in 1652 when Leibniz was 6 years old. His mother dedicated herself to the upbringing and education of her only son and his sister. Leibniz loved learning. When he was 8 years old, he studied two Latin books left lying around in the house by a student lodger. A friend of the family was so impressed by Leibniz's self-taught knowledge that he made the family promise to let the boy have free range of his father's library. The young Leibniz read an enormous amount in almost all areas of knowledge. He mastered Latin, and studied Greek and Scholastic philosophy. Later in life, he described himself as almost self-taught.

Leibniz began to discover his path in life when he learned Aristotelian logic in the last years of high school. He was especially interested in Aristotle's categories as a means of organizing knowledge. Through this study, Leibniz discovered his idea of an alphabet of human thought, or the idea that, by having a complete set of simple concepts, all truths could be demonstrated. The elaboration of this idea was one of Leibniz's primary life works and it influenced his mathematics, logic, and metaphysics.

In 1661, at the age of 15, he entered the university of Leipzig to study philosophy and later jurisprudence. His undergraduate thesis was entitled *Metaphysical Disputation on the Principle of Individuation.* In this early work, we find the principle that was so important for his later metaphysics: that all individuals are individuated by their totality.

It was around this time that Leibniz became acquainted with modern philosophy and he felt that he had to choose between the moderns and the scholastics. Walking in the gardens of Rosenthal in the outskirts of Leipzig, he opted for the modern mechanistic philosophy and, because of this choice, he decided to study mathematics.

In 1666, when Leibniz was 20, the university refused to award him the doctorate in law because of his young age and so the student moved to the University of Altdorf in Nuremberg, where he was awarded the doctorate the following year. His doctoral thesis, entitled *On Difficult Cases in Law,* was published in 1669.

Around this time, Leibniz decided to learn some alchemy. When he found that he could not penetrate its mysteries, he compiled a list of the more obscure terms in alchemy. Using these expressions that he himself could not understand, he wrote a letter to the director of the secret society claiming profound knowledge of alchemy. The ruse worked. He was accepted into the society and was even offered a salary to work as the secretary. This story shows the complete confidence

3

Leibniz had in his own abilities, which is a characteristic of his whole life.

1. Mainz

In 1667 Leibniz met Baron von Boineburg, who was the chief minister of the Elector of Mainz. The Baron was very impressed by the young man and sought a position for him in the service of the Elector. Leibniz was also offered a professorship at Altdorf which he refused, accepting instead the post as assistant to the legal advisor of the Elector. Leibniz spent the rest of his life working for princes and dukes.

As a result of this position, Leibniz wrote several legal works, including *A New Method for Teaching and Learning Jurisprudence,* which contained a list of what was missing in the law. In addition, he wrote a project to reform German law, a confused mixture of Roman law, common law and the laws of the various Germanic states. To systematize the legal system, he hoped to define all legal concepts in terms of a few basic principles, a vision of the law harking back to his idea of the alphabet of human thought.

During this period Leibniz began to develop his plan for a universal system of knowledge. This vision affected his work as the librarian for Baron von Boineburg. Using the Baron's large collection as a model, Leibniz made a catalogue of the books according to their subject matter, something quite novel for the time. He asked for permission to do the same for other major libraries, but was always refused. He also conceived a central publication that would have an abstract of all serious new books to help librarians choose their purchases, but twice his application for a licence was turned down.

In 1669, Leibniz wrote a short treatise attempting to solve the problem of the Polish Royal succession. In 1668, the King of Poland had abdicated and there were several pretenders to the throne. Leibniz's solution was to argue that Poland should become a republic and elect one of these pretenders to lead it.

Around this time, Leibniz wrote a paper for Boineburg, entitled *Confessions of Nature against Atheists,* which attempts to prove the existence of God and the immortality of the soul. He composed this paper in an inn and sent it to von Boineburg without signing it. The theologian Spitzel published the piece in 1669, not knowing who the author was. Leibniz also wrote *Defence of the Trinity* at the request of von Boineburg, who was a Catholic and a keen promoter of the reunion of the Catholic and Lutheran churches in Germany. This project of unification became an important lifelong project of Leibniz's.

4

In 1670, Leibniz published his first work in philosophy - a preface and some notes to a reprint of a book written by the Italian humanist, Marius Nizolius in 1553. In his work, Nizolius attacks the scholastics and Aristotle, who had dominated philosophy for centuries. In this introduction, Leibniz shows that he does not rebel radically against his scholastic background. As we shall see, this is a characteristic that distinguishes him from other modern philosophers.

In 1671, Leibniz published his first work in natural philosophy or physics. The work, *A New Physical Hypothesis*, consists of two parts. Leibniz dedicated the first part, *The Abstract Theory of Motion*, to the Academy of Paris. The second, *The Concrete Theory of Motion*, he dedicated and sent to the Royal Society of London. Because of his broad interests, Leibniz was keen to join such research societies and hence his dedications which were later to bear fruit. Later still, Leibniz was to form his own academies.

The main medium of intellectual exchange during this time was private correspondence. Leibniz was an enthusiastic letter writer, as was his patron von Boineburg, who put Leibniz in contact with intellectuals from all over Europe. In this way Leibniz developed a circle of hundreds of correspondents. He assiduously preserved copies of his own letters. Fifteen thousand of them still survive, and it is through these, as well as his personal notes, that we know much about his philosophy.

Leibniz also worked to resolve the French threat to Germany after the Thirty Years' War. Under Louis XIV, France was a united country and the major power on the continent of Europe. In contrast, what we now call Germany consisted of hundreds of states all owing allegiance to the Emperor of the Holy Roman Empire. Leibniz devised various schemes to weaken the French economy, such as destroying the French trade in brandy with cheaper rum based on West Indies sugar. He produced a plan for France to invade Egypt and wage war against the "infidels", in order to distract Louis XIV away from Germany. Von Boineburg liked the plan and, in the spring of 1672, he sent Leibniz to Paris to sell it to the French.

2. Paris

Soon after arriving in Paris, Leibniz made friends with the famous philosophers Arnauld and Malebranche, and the mathematician Huygens. He was able to gain access to the unpublished works of Descartes and Pascal. Some of Descartes' works only exist because of the copies made by Leibniz.

Germany was backward in mathematics compared to Paris and Leibniz soon realized that he had a lot to learn. Far from being discouraged, he studied under the guidance of Huygens and made the important mathematical discoveries which later led him into rivalry with Newton.

Leibniz's original purpose in coming to Paris never came to fruition. Nevertheless, he remained there with an official post until 1676, when he was 30. This seems to have been the period of Leibniz's life during which his own views began to take shape.

In January 1673, he was sent to London where he made contact with the secretary of the Royal Society. Leibniz was able to show the members of the Society his proto-type for a mechanical calculator, which was able to multiply and divide. Since at the time few educated people could actually multiply, this invention was quite an achievement. Moreover, it was a big improvement on the earlier version of an adding machine made by Pascal in 1642. In 1673, Leibniz was elected member of the Royal Society, because his machine was acknowledged as one of the great inventions of the time. A model of it can be seen in Hanover's central library. Leibniz dreamed of a much larger machine which could be used to mechanize all reasoning and he planned a system for giving all possible thoughts a number.

Leibniz also designed several other inventions during this period of his life. They included: a compressed-air engine, a ship that could travel underwater, an aneroid barometer, a device for calculating the position of a ship without a compass or observing the stars, and improvements to lenses.

His stay in London was terminated by the news of the death of his two sponsors: Baron von Boineburg and the Elector of Mainz. He returned to Paris and continued his work tutoring von Boineburg's son until 1676. Leibniz hankered after a job as a research fellow of the Paris Academy, but no such offer was made to him, and so he accepted work as Court Councillor in Hanover. In October 1676, he returned to Germany via Holland and spent four days in discussions with the famous philosopher Spinoza.

3. Hanover

In Hanover, as well as acting as councillor to the court, Leibniz worked as head librarian for his new employer, Duke Friedrich, who had a huge collection of books and manuscripts. In 1679, the whole collection was transferred from the Palace to a new building in the center of Hanover. The library was moved again in 1681. Finally, in 1698, it was relocated to its permanent home in the Leibniz-haus (which was rebuilt after being destroyed in World War II) .

Leibniz sent memoranda to the Duke recommending changes in public administration, as well as suggesting comprehensive economic surveys and economic councils to promote trade and training. He also recommended that the Duke establish a department for state archives, with handbooks containing regulations and indeces of archival papers.

In 1679, Leibniz proposed to the Duke the idea that wind power could be used to drain the silver mines in the Harz mountains. Later, he designed many kinds of windmills, pumps and gear mechanisms. Leibniz hoped that the money from the mines would help establish and fund an academic society, which would in turn make his main project possible - the encyclopedia for the universal language. He realized that an academy would require a source of income. For the next nine years, he spent half his time in the mountains trying to make these various inventions work. They did not succeed and Leibniz claimed that his inventions had been blocked by administrators and others fearful that the new technology would result in fewer jobs.

Leibniz also submitted plans for many other technological projects. Some were related to mining, such as ore carriers and improvements to the methods of steel making. Others were not related to mining, such as methods for manufacturing porcelain and linen, plans for canals and water desalination.

Leibniz also served as a diplomat. In 1676, he published a treatise defending the right of German states to be treated as sovereign and not merely as vassals of the Emperor.

One of his life's missions was to reconcile the Lutheran and the Catholic churches in Germany. Previously, Leibniz had written some papers for von Boineburg concerning the Trinity and arguing against atheism and materialism. In 1679, he offered to write a work which would serve as a theology for both Protestants and Catholics. Before embarking on this project, he sought assurance from the Vatican that his interpretations of crucial theological points would not be considered heresy. The project was halted because of the death of his patron, Duke Friedrich, in December 1679. Leibniz, who composed verse in Latin and French, wrote a poem in Latin to commemorate the death of his patron.

4. Brunswick

Ernst Augusto, the younger brother, was the successor to the Duke Friedrich. In August 1685, it was clear that Leibniz's drainage plans for the mines would not succeed and Augusto asked Leibniz to write a history of the whole Guelf family from earliest times to the present. In December 1686, Leibniz accepted. To research the family history, he travelled in Bavaria, Austria and Italy from November 1687 to June 1690, using the opportunity to become acquainted with other scholars and to become elected a member of the Academy of Rome. During this time, there occurred a little adventure that is poignant. Leibniz was traveling as the only passenger on a small boat near Venice. During a storm, the sailors openly planned to throw him overboard and steal his things. Leibniz pretended not to have understood them and quietly got out a rosary and pretended to pray. Thinking that Leibniz was Catholic, the sailors changed their minds.

In 1690, Leibniz returned to Hanover with a vast collection of archival material related to the history which he published in six large volumes in 1698-1700 and in three volumes related specifically to the Guelfs in 1707-11. Other volumes were published after his death. However, Leibniz regarded this historical work as a burden, like the stone of Sisyphus. In 1695, he described his life as full of distractions. While he was forced to search for documents for the history, he had many new ideas concerning mathematics and philosophy, which he had no time to develop. Indeed, in 1697, he expressed the wish that if death would allow him the time to accomplish all his projects, then he would promise to start no new ones. Leibniz was described by his biographer Eckhart as a person who would never give up. For example, in 1694, he hired a skilled workman to produce a working model of his calculating machine (capable of multiplying figures of 12 digits), and yet again he tried to introduce new pumps and water power into the mines of Harz.

Leibniz wrote two preliminary essays for the Guelf family history. The first, called *Protogaea*, is a work on geology, concerning the formation of fossils and minerals. The second essay concerns the migration of European tribes. Leibniz gathered a huge amount of data concerning the origins of European languages.

In fact, Leibniz never completed the history. He was a man who liked to be paid well, and he acquired other part-time appointments including the care of the Augusta Library at Wolfenbüttel. He was also receiving a salary from Duke Wilhelm of Celle. For this part of his life, Leibniz divided his time between, on the one hand, Celle, Brunswick, Wolfenbüttel and, on the other, Hanover. Because of these commitments, he spent a lot of time travelling by coach.

5. Hanover

Ernst Augusto died in 1698 and was succeeded by his eldest son, George Ludwig, who was now Leibniz's employer and who had much less sympathy for Leibniz's habit of working on so many projects at the same time. He complained about the philosopher's many "invisible books." His main concern was that his employee finish the family history.

By around 1700, Leibniz saw himself as an expert on succession. He wrote pamphlets on every important case, such as the succession to the Spanish and Austrian thrones after the death of Charles II of Spain in 1700. He was invited by George Ludwig's sister to have her husband appointed King of Prussia. He was especially interested in the succession to the English throne. The Bill of Rights passed in 1689 prohibited a Catholic from inheriting the English throne, and consequently the succession passed through James I's daughter, Elizabeth of Bohemia, to her grandson, George Ludwig, Leibniz's employer. However, there were many delicate negotiations between Hanover and London before Ludwig's succession in 1714, when he became George I. Additionally, Leibniz persuaded Anton Ulrich of Brunswick to drop his claim to the Electorate of the German Empire. In 1708, he tried to obtain the Bishopric of Hildesheim for the Duke of Brunswick.

Leibniz was very active promoting scientific societies around this time. In 1700, he was the founding president of the Berlin Society of Sciences, later known as the Prussian Academy. He tried to form a similar academy in Dresden. Realizing that the Berlin Society would need money to operate, Leibniz tried to find income. He proposed, among other ideas, the cultivation of silk-worms. He gained the patent for silk in Prussia and advocated that mulberry bushes be planted.

In 1712, he was made an Imperial councillor in Vienna and appointed director of the academy, which did not open until after his death. A similar academy in Russia was again not opened until after he had died. By 1712, he was employed by five European courts: Hanover, Brunswick, Berlin, Vienna and St. Petersburg. This meant, of course, that he was travelling a lot and that he had trouble satisfying his employers, especially the court of Hanover, which was still waiting for the history of the Guelf family.

In 1714, George Ludwig moved to England to become king. Leibniz was now too old to travel much and he stayed in Hanover working on the unfinished history, which he hoped to complete so that he could write a major philosophical work afterwards. At the same time, he was considering moving to Paris, London, Berlin and even St. Petersburg. He wrote some of his most important philosophical correspondence during this period. On November 14th 1716, at the age of 70, Leibniz died.

In summary, Leibniz must have had a very quick and incredibly active mind. His notes "reveal an impatient intellect hurrying to express its ideas as quickly as possible" (p.70 Jolley ed., 1995). He would work

9

for months without leaving his study. He designed a coach for himself so that he could write while travelling. Yet he complained of a thousand distractions (G iii 194). Why was his life at times like this? First, being so optimistic and persistent, he would not give up a project once he had begun it. We have seen this pattern repeated throughout his life. Second, Leibniz had four major patrons: Baron von Boineburg, Duke Friedrich, Ernst Augusto, George Ludwig. Each was successively less sympathetic to Leibniz's main cause, his plan for a universal language and, as a consequence, in part to please his patrons, Leibniz became embroiled in many other projects, such as the mines, the history and various political schemes. Third, we must consider Leibniz's own vanity which lead him to have so many employers. The Duchess of Orleans said of Leibniz as a young man: "it is so rare for intellectuals to be smartly dressed and not to smell and to understand jokes" (p26, Ross). As an old man, he was sometimes ridiculed for his ornate and old fashioned mode of dress. Last, but not least, we must remember Leibniz's wide sense of charity and care for humanity, which motivated all of his work. He himself wrote:

> Provided that something of importance is achieved, I am indifferent whether it is done in Germany or in France, for I seek the good of mankind (p39, Riley).

2
A New Approach

In Leibniz's philosophical work, we can see the qualities of a diplomat, mathematician, and inventor. However, of these, perhaps the diplomat is the most prominent. He is the grand reconciler of views. He tries to reconcile atomism and Cartensianism, mechanism and vitalism, as well as scholastism and modern philosophy. (As we shall see later, two other characteristics of Leibniz as a person that influence his style of doing philosophy are his benevolence and his optimism.)

Leibniz's university teacher at Leipzig, Jacob Thomasius, belonged to a group of thinkers who had a distinctive philosophical approach. They believed that Aristotle (384-322 B.C.) had been badly misunderstood by the medieval scholastic philosophers and that important insights could be gained by "rediscovering" the thought of Aristotle. Furthermore, this group practised an eclectic approach to philosophy, according to which one attained a true vision of philosophy by combining the work of very different philosophical traditions into one coherent system. Leibniz inherited this way of working and, thanks to this, he looked as far away as China for insight.

In this spirit of reconciliation, Leibniz asserts:

> I have found that most sects are correct in the better part of what they put forward, though not so much in what they deny (Letter to Remond, 10 January 1714)

and

> Our greatest failure has been the sectarian spirit which imposes limits upon itself by spurning others (Loemker, p. 496).

11

These quotes express one of the distinctive features of Leibniz's philosophical approach. By combining the positive insights of different traditions into a coherent whole, and by trying to overcome the apparent inconsistencies between them, one can arrive at the true philosophy. In particular, modern, mechanistic philosophers are mistaken to reject wholesale Aristotelian thought. There must be a way to combine the two.

Furthermore, according to Leibniz, this reconciliation contains the secret to resolving the religious and political conflicts of the time. He lived during a time of political disunity, caused by religious disharmony, which in turn was due to philosophical conflict. Leibniz dreamed of a Europe at peace and thought that the main obstacle to this was the schism between the Protestant and Catholic churches. The impediment to church reunification concerned certain points of doctrine, such as transubstantiation, which could be overcome by good philosophy. In particular, modern philosophy mistakenly had tried to abandon its scholastic roots.

The Road to Metaphysics

As a young adult, Leibniz had three fundamental projects. The first was to develop the idea of his youth: the alphabet of human thought. This led him to work in logic throughout his adult life and to think about the nature of the proposition and the concept of truth. It was this project which led Leibniz to conceive all knowledge in an encyclopedic form. He planned an encyclopedia, entitled *Plus ultra,* for which he wrote many introductory pieces and papers on logic. In later life, this project inspired him to work on forming academies, which in turn led him to work on income-generating projects, such as the Harz mines and the silk farms.

His second life-long project was concerned with physics. Leibniz was unhappy with both of the major modern schools of physics: atomism and Cartesianism. His work in the mathematics of calculus had led him to think deeply about the implications of the infinite divisibility of matter. Neither of the two modern schools of thought dealt adequately with this point, because both ignored Aristotle's work on substance and its relation to motion.

Leibniz's third fundamental project was to bridge the schism between the Catholic and Protestant churches. Encouraged by his first patron, Baron von Boinberg, Leibniz started work on his essay, the *Catholic Demonstrations*, in 1668; this was his first step in his life-long project of unifying the two churches. In this, Leibniz was in part motivated by the political turmoil of the time which had its roots in the religious divisions. Leibniz thought that these in turn were based on philosophical misunderstandings, and therefore he sought to clarify theology. Of course, even in his early adult life, Leibniz had other projects apart from these three. However, these three are the most fundamental to the development of his thought. As he worked more deeply in each one of these projects, they pointed more and more towards common metaphysical conclusions. In a large part, Leibniz's mature metaphysics grew from these three schemes.

Substance

However, there is one further element which needs mentioning: Leibniz's interest from a very early age in the principle of individuation, which was the subject of his undergraduate thesis. The question that motivates this topic is: 'What does reality actually consist of?" The Aristotelian answer is that reality consists primarily of substances. This simple answer provides a framework for Leibniz's thinking about metaphysics during his whole life. The simple answer implies that to learn about the nature of reality, one needs to understand properly the concept of a substance and, in particular, how substances should be individuated from each other. To discover what reality consists of, we have to find out what kinds of things have non-derivative existence. Certain phenomena, such as smiles and laughs, only exist insofar as other more fundamental things exist, such as people who smile and laugh. By definition, substance has non-derivative existence.

As we shall see, Leibniz's mature metaphysics paints an original and extraordinary picture of reality. In broad outline, it "represents an important, permanent metaphysical alternative, one of the handful of fundamental views in this area that has a real chance of being true" (Adams, 1994, p.5). To understand this system, we need to follow the arguments which support his metaphysical conclusions. In this we find three difficulties. First, Leibniz's claims about language and truth, matter and space, and mind and reality are very tightly interconnected. They are like a compressed ball of string and, for this reason, it is difficult to separate the lines or threads of reasoning. Second, his views change during his lifetime. Third, much of his philosophy is contained in journals and letters, rather than in books. His main metaphysical works are:

Discourse on Metaphysics	1686
New System	1695

In large part, Leibniz's metaphysics can be seen as a confluence of, first, his work on logic and language; second, his work on physics; third, his thinking regarding biology and psychology. In this book we shall represent his metaphysics of substance through seven steps.

1. All propositions are, or are reducible to, subject-predicate form (chapter 4)
2. Truth is the containment of the predicate concept in the subject concept (chapter 4)
3. Substance cannot be divisible (the problem of the continuum) (chapter 5)
4. Mechanical science requires the postulation of an active force (chapter 5)
5. Space and time are relational and not absolute (chapter 6)
6. The principle of continuity: nature never makes leaps (chapter 7)
7. Substance must be self-contained (chapter 7)

These different elements of Leibniz's thought (his views of language, physics, psychology and biology) converge to produce a remarkable metaphysics, which we will review in chapters 8 and 9.

3
Logic:
The Alphabet of Thought

The idea of an alphabet of human thought consists of two claims: first, that all concepts are either simple or complex; and second, that the latter are composed out of the former. Given this, if we could discover the simple elements (vocabulary) and the rules according to which they are combined (syntax), then we would understand the composition of human thought. In this way, it might be possible to explain the human mind, and even the universe, as a machine. Leibniz adopted Hobbes' comment that all reasoning is calculation. He hoped to develop a universal language that would make all reasoning transparently clear. Such a language would be a powerful tool for reasoning, comparable to the microscope for seeing. It is with these ideas in mind that Leibniz invented his calculating machines, and it is these hopes that motivated most of his work in logic, and his attempts to establish academic societies in order to find collaborators to work on the encyclopedic project.

The Art of Combination

In 1666, at the age of 20, Leibniz wrote the *Dissertation on the Art of Combination,* to gain a position teaching philosophy at the University of Leipzig. The content of this treatise is the theory of combinations and permutations as applied to propositions, which forms a general method for forming all propositions. Leibniz devised the mathematics of both permutations and combinations which, unknown to him, had already been discovered.

However, more important is the application of this method to human thought. Leibniz assumes that all propositions have a subject-predicate form, a fundamental assumption that he held all of his life (see chapter 4). Suppose that there are four simple concepts represented by 3,6,7, and 9. A second class of concepts can be formed by combining these four in different arrangements: 3.6, 3.7, 3.9, 6.7 , 6.9, 7.9. A third class would consist of propositions represented numerically with three numerals, such as 3.6.9. and so on. In this way, we can construct complex concepts from simple ones by a rule of combination similar to multiplication. For example, Leibniz represents 'interval is the total space included' as 'interval is 2.3.10.' He compares this way of representing propositions to Chinese in which the combination of ideas is visibly shown.

Leibniz thought of this work as the first step towards the universal system that he was seeking. He was confident that in principle all propositions could be represented in this universal form, because of his claim that all propositions have a subject-predicate form. Propositions, such as 'the leaf is green', have a subject-predicate form because they predicate a property ('is green') to a subject ('the leaf'). The statement that all propositions have this form entails that relational terms, prepositions, tenses and articles do not represent fundamental items. The next step was to show how reasoning could function as a calculus analogous to arithmetic.

A Calculus for Propositions

Leibniz was fond of the saying of St. Augustine:

> Do not permit yourself to think you have known truth in philosophy unless you can explain the leap in which we deduce that one, two, three and four together make ten (Brown, p55).

To explain a logical truth, one must be able to prove it. Proving it consists in deducing it from certain definitions and self-evident axioms, using what is now sometimes called Leibniz's law, which states that identical expressions can be substituted. For example, '2+1' may be substituted for '3' in any formula, and '4' can be replaced by '3+1.' In this way we can prove that 2+2=4, for, by substitution, we can show that this is equivalent to '3+1=3+1.' This is the way to answer St. Augustine's challenge.

Leibniz considers the above example to be a simple model for all reasoning. In principle, all logical truths can be demonstrated in a similar fashion. For example, if the definition of the word 'human' is 'rational animal' then, we can demonstrate that humans are rational because such a proposition becomes 'ab is a' (where 'a' is 'rational' and 'b' is 'animal'). Leibniz extends this idea to all propositions, and we shall explain this in the next chapter. In this way, the alphabet of human thought would be a powerful tool of logical demonstration that would end disputes. It would allow us to calculate without having to pay attention to the meaning of what is written, once we have the appropriate definitions.

Leibniz realizes that these ideas are the seeds of a huge research project rather than only a definitive philosophical position. First, it requires showing how language can be idealized to fit into the required subject-predicate form. For example, in three papers written in 1678, Leibniz tries to show that conjugations, gender and declensions can be ignored. He proposes to treat most nouns as adjectives governing the words 'entity' or 'subject', so , for example, the noun 'human' would be 'the subject of humanity.' He also tries to show how relational statements can be eliminated from a "rational grammar."

Second, the project points to the need for a dictionary of definitions, and perhaps even a whole encyclopedia, in order to construct the vocabulary of the language from the required primitive concepts. Leibniz realized that he could not undertake such a work on his own, and this is in part why he was in contact with the secretaries of learned societies or academies, and why later in life, he was active in promoting such societies. As late as 1704, he was working on this project: in that year his secretary completed the alphabetical lexicon, which consisted in five tables of definitions.

Third, as a necessary part of this overall program, Leibniz tries to find numerical methods for representing logical inferences. In a series of papers written from 1679 to 1690, he attempts to represent logical inferences in numerical terms. Over the years he experimented with several different methods of trying to make logical deduction into a numerical calculation.

In 1679, he wrote three papers, including *Elements of a Calculus*, adopting the principle that the composition of complex concepts is analogous to multiplication. Another paper of that year represents concepts by a pair of numbers. If the concept of an animal is represent by $+13$, -5 and 'rational' by $+8,-7$ then 'human' would be the product of these, i.e. $+104$, -35. By such a method all possible thoughts can be represented mathematically as functions of simple concepts.

This effort over several years culminated in a paper of 1690, called *A Study in the Calculus of Real Addition*, in which he represents the combination of the concepts A and B not by AB, but by A $\oplus$ B (p. 131, ed. Parkinson, 1966). This new notation signals that $\oplus$ is different from +. For instance, 'A $\oplus$ A = A' is an axiom of this system. 'A $\oplus$ B = L' means that L is composed of B and A. For instance, the concept of a human is composed of the concepts 'rational' and 'animal'. It implies that the concept of A is contained in that of L.

This work can be seen as an attempt to produce a purely formal deductive system, similar to the system developed by Boole (1815-64) In his work, Leibniz deduces 24 propositions from various definitions and axioms. For example, proposition 4 states that if A=B and B$\neq$C then A$\neq$C. Proposition 5 says that if A is in B and if A=C then C is in B. Proposition 15 asserts: If A is in B and B is in C then A is in C Proposition 20: If A is in M and B is in N, then A$\oplus$B will be in M$\oplus$N.

Interpretation

This is the first attempt at a purely formal calculus. Leibniz realizes that the equations and symbols can be given different interpretations because of their abstract nature. He says:

> Therefore, the whole of synthesis and analysis depends upon the principles laid down here (Parkinson, p.142)

For instance, the symbols representing combinations can be given an intensional and an extensional interpretation. An extensional interpretation of A$\oplus$B = L would imply that the class A$\oplus$B includes all the members of the class of L. This is extensional because it concerns the extension or scope of the relevant terms. For instance, the class 'rational $\oplus$ animal' includes the class 'human'. So, under this interpretation, we would say that the class of animals includes the class of humans, or that A includes L. In contrast, according to the intensional interpretation, A$\oplus$B = L would imply that the concept of L includes the concept of A$\oplus$B. This is intensional because it concerns intensions or concepts. Under this interpretation, we would say that the concept of human includes the concept of animal, or that L includes A. Under one interpretation A includes L, and under the other, L includes A.

Leibniz is aware of the differences between the intensional and extensional views of propositions, and generally favors the intensional view on the grounds that to assert a proposition is to say that one concept is included in another. This view implies that propositions such as 'all unicorns have horns' can be true even though there are no unicorns. This point will become important later.

Binary Mathematics

During his time in Paris (1672-6), Leibniz made his most important mathematical discoveries, including the differential and integral calculus, which we shall discuss in the appendix to chapter 5. He also developed binary arithmetic, which is a number system based on only two numerals, zero and one. In the binary system, '2' is written as '10' and '4' as '100'. Leibniz, of course, did not realize that this system would become the basis for the modern computer. Nevertheless, he considered the idea of expressing his logical calculus in binary numbers (the numbers generated would have been unimaginably complex). In about 1680, he also sketched a design for a calculating machine to work in binary numbers. Of course, such a machine would have to have a great number of wheels and, for this reason, he abandoned the plan. He came as close as anyone could to inventing the computer.

During his lifetime, Leibniz never published any paper or treatise on logic and, yet in the twentieth century, he has been recognized as one of the pioneers of logic. For example, he developed what were later called Euler circles or Venn diagrams to represent logical relations. He also gave an explanation of identity, or =, similar to contemporary accounts. More than anything, he developed an abstract logical calculus and, because of this, we call him the first symbolic logician.

In conclusion, Leibniz's project of the alphabet of human thought led him to develop something almost equivalent to a formal logical system. It also led him to his theory of truth as concept inclusion and to his theory of substance individuation.

4
Truth and Substance

In the course of his writings on logic, Leibniz develops a theory of the proposition, which has two parts: the definition of truth and the claim that the subject–predicate form of proposition is basic. Since he defines a true proposition as one in which the subject concept contains the predicate concept, the definition of truth requires the view that all propositions are reducible to the subject–predicate form. If there were some propositions not reducible to this form, then Leibniz's definition of truth would not be applicable to them.

The Subject-Predicate Form

Leibniz claims that the subject–predicate form of proposition is basic. In other words, all other types of proposition can be reduced to this form. In a subject–predicate proposition, a property is affirmed or denied of the subject of the proposition, such as 'water is wet.' In this example, the subject term is 'water' and the predicate is 'is wet.'

Obviously, not all propositions are of this grammatical form. For example, hypothetical propositions, such as 'if it is Friday, then we should go to the bank,' are not. Neither are relational propositions, such as 'the tree is to the left of the bush'. However, Leibniz claims that these other types of propositions can be reduced to those that are of the subject-predicate form. For example, hypothetical propositions, such as `If anything is a human then it is an animal' are of the form 'If p then q.' Nevertheless, they can be reduced to the subject–predicate form, for example: 'The concept of humanity contains the concept of being an animal'.

This point about language has important implications. The metaphysical counterpart of subject–predicate propositions are substances and their properties. If subject–predicate propositions are basic, then reality can be completely described with this type of proposition. This means that reality ultimately consists only of substances and their properties. This last point implies that spatio–temporal relations between substances are not an additional item in the universe, as we shall see later.

The Nature of Truth

The second part of Leibniz's theory of the proposition is an analysis of truth. What is it that makes a proposition true? According to Leibniz, a proposition is true if and only if the predicate-concept of the proposition is contained in the subject-concept. For example, in the proposition 'the hairless man is bald', the idea of the subject ('the hairless man') contains the predicate concept ('is bald') very obviously. The one entails the other.

According to Leibniz, in all true propositions the concept of the subject contains the predicate, even when this entailment is not at all obvious. So, for example, the proposition 'Washington is the first US president' is true because the concept of Washington contains or logically entails the predicate concept (i.e. 'is the first president'), even though this entailment is not obvious.

This analysis of truth in terms of concept inclusion has the consequence that all true propositions are analytic. Against the charge that many true propositions are not analytic, Leibniz defends his analysis of truth by distinguishing three different kinds of analytic propositions.

1) A proposition, such as 'a male is a male', is self–evidently analytic; it is a statement of identity of the form 'A is A', which cannot be denied without immediate self–contradiction.

2) Other propositions, such as 'the hairless man is bald,' 'my brother is a male' and 'a triangle has three sides', can be shown to be statements of identity (of the form 'A is A') by a finite process of analysis. For instance, analysis of the concept of a triangle shows us

21

that, by definition, a triangle is a two dimensional figure with three sides. Consequently, the proposition 'a triangle has three sides' can be shown to be a statement of identity by a finite process of analysis. It has the form 'A is A'. Once the concept of a triangle is properly understood, it becomes self–evident that the proposition 'the triangle has three sides' is a statement of identity and hence analytic.

3) Other true propositions, such as 'Julius Caesar died in 49 BC.' do not appear to be statements of identity. They do not appear to be so, but this is only because we do not know their full infinite analysis. Leibniz claims that such propositions really are statements of identity, and that if the concept of Julius Caesar were properly understood, it would be self–evident that the proposition 'Julius Caesar died in 49 BC.' is a statement of identity. The reason why it does not appear so to us is that we are incapable of completing the infinite analysis of the concept of Julius Caesar, which is known only to God.

In summary, Leibniz claims that in all true propositions the subject contains the predicate. This analysis of truth implies that all true propositions are statements of identity and are analytic. Leibniz defends this claim by arguing that we should distinguish two kinds of propositions: those, such as 'the triangle has three sides' which are explicitly analytic and those, such as 'Caesar died in 49 BC.' which are implicitly analytic.

The Principle of Sufficient Reason

The Principle of Sufficient Reason is a corollary of this theory of truth. The principle affirms that for every fact there must be a sufficient reason why things are so and not otherwise. Everything must have a cause, and 'cause' means a sufficient reason.

The Principle of Sufficient Reason follows from the definition of truth. This is because stating a reason for the truth of any proposition consists of giving an a priori proof of that proposition; all propositions have an a priori proof, and this is what is meant by the saying that nothing happens without a cause. The a priori proof of a proposition must consist of demonstrating the logical connection between the subject and its predicate. Therefore, because of his definition of truth, all propositions have an a priori proof, and thus the Principle of Sufficient Reason is true.

Primitive Concepts

22

Leibniz's project of 'the alphabet of human thoughts' is intimately connected to his theory of truth. He compares the formation of complex concepts from their primitive constituents to the way in which words are formed by the combination of letters. For example, the concept of a bachelor is a combination of the concepts of man and unmarried; the concept of a man is a combination of the concepts of male and human, and so on. Even though we are not aware of it, our normal concepts are simply combinations of primitive concepts.

The concept of Julius Caesar is such a combination. This is why we are not aware that the proposition 'Caesar died in 49 BC.' is in reality a statement of identity. The concept of Caesar already contains the predicate 'died in 49 BC.', because all the primitive concepts which constitute the concept of Julius Caesar include those primitive concepts which make up the predicate. In effect, the complete concept of Julius Caesar is a combination of simple concepts which can be represented by a string of letters 'ABCDE....'. When we say that Caesar died on a particular day, we are saying something which is already included in the list, and can be represented as 'ABCDE .... is A'.

What argument does Leibniz give for the claim that all propositions are really identical? He argues that the complete concept of Caesar must contain all the predicates true of that man because an individual substance can be individuated completely only by all of its properties. In other words, Leibniz argues that his theory of truth is required by the nature of substance.

The Identity of Substances

Leibniz defines a substance as a subject to which many predicates can be attributed, but which cannot itself be made the predicate of any other subject. For insance, the individual soul is a substance, and this means that the soul is the subject of properties, but is not itself the property or attribute of any subject. On the other hand, redness is not a substance, because it is the property or attribute of red things.

According to Leibniz, the concept of every individual substance is completely determinate. The complete concept of the individual substance contains every fact about that substance right down to the most minute detail. From the complete concept of any substance, it is possible to infer all the properties of that substance.

Every predicate must be contained in the subject, because otherwise we would be unable to distinguish an individual from all other possible individuals. For instance, there are many possible individuals who could have been called 'Adam', and who could have led almost identical lives to Adam himself. Leibniz calls these possible individuals "several alternative possible Adams." Suppose Adam did in fact exist, then, according to Leibniz, the only description which would suffice to describe him as a completely unique individual, distinct from all other possible individuals, would be the description which specifies the complete notion of Adam, i.e., the sum total of all his predicates.

Consequently, the thesis that every predicate must be contained in the subject is based on his view about what individuates a substance. A substance is defined and individuated from all other possible individual substances by the sum total of all its predicates. If any one of the predicates were different, the individual would be a different individual. In other words, the thesis that all the properties of an individual substance are essential properties entails that every predicate is contained in the subject.

These points require the distinction between the concept of Caesar and a concept of Caesar. To have the concept of Caesar, it is necessary to have complete knowledge of him and every detail of his life, and consequently, only God can have it. Finite minds, like ours, can only have a partial and incomplete concept of any individual such as Caesar and consequently, we cannot see that true propositions such as 'Caesar died in 49 BC.' are indeed identical or of the form 'A is A'. Thus, only God can see that the concept of Julius Caesar includes and entails every predicate that is true of the man.

In summary, Leibniz thinks that every substance must have a complete concept. Because the concept of a substance is complete, whatever can be truly said of that substance must be contained in the concept of that substance. He argues that the complete concept of a substance is both necessary and sufficient to identify that individual substance and to distinguish it from all other possible individuals. Because the complete concept of a substance is both necessary and sufficient to distinguish it from all other possible individuals, no two individuals share the same complete concept. This means that no two individuals can be exactly alike. This result is called the Principle of the Identity of Indiscernibles, and it follows from the claim that each substance must have a complete concept.

The Identity of Indiscernibles

The principle states that numerically different individuals must be qualitatively dissimilar. Since there cannot be two substances with the same complete concept, there cannot be two substances that are exactly alike. So stated, the principle putatively expresses a necessary truth: it is self–contradictory to suppose that there might be two qualitatively identical individuals. Indeed, the Identity of Indiscernibles must be a necessary truth because it follows from the assertion that each substance must have a complete concept, and this is a necessary truth.

However, in his fifth letter to Clarke, Leibniz suggests that the Principle of the Identity of the Indiscernibles is contingent. In the letter, he claims it is not absolutely necessary to suppose that there cannot be two exactly similar individuals, but rather that such a supposition is contrary to the will of God: we can be certain of this because everything must have a sufficient reason and God could not have a sufficient reason for creating two identical individuals. Suppose, for example, that there are two qualitatively identical individual bodies, A and B and God fills one space with A and another space with B. Leibniz argues against Clarke that, in such a case, which body fills which space would be arbitrary, or without reason. Since everything must have a reason, there cannot be two such bodies. In this way, the Principle of the Identity of Indiscernibles is required by the Principle of Sufficient Reason. This is an important conclusion for Leibniz's view on space.

Sometimes Leibniz appeals to the empirical claim that one will always be able to find qualitative differences between two individuals, however much alike they may seem at first sight. But once again, this suggests that the Principle of the Identity of Indiscernibles is contingent.

Is the Principle of the Identity of Indiscernibles true? Could two individuals with identical properties possibly exist? Arguably the principle is true if we allow spatial and temporal relations to count towards the properties of a substance, and if we assume that two things cannot be in the same place at the same time. Suppose we have two billiard balls, which are exactly alike with respect to shape, size, color and texture. Since they cannot occupy the same place at the same time, then they must have different spatial and temporal relations or positions. If we include these relations and positions among their respective properties, then the two objects cannot be indiscernible.

Leibniz, however, does not regard spatial objects as substances, and he claims that all relations can be reduced to qualitative predicates, or intrinsic denominations. These points we shall explain later. For these reasons, he cannot include spatial and temporal relations among the properties of a substance. Thus, Leibniz argues that two substances cannot differ solely with respect to their spatio–temporal relations and positions. If they differ in this way, then this must be because they differ with respect to their intrinsic properties.

Necessary and Contingent Truths

25

It seems that the definition of truth implies that all truths are necessary. The concept of a substance contains the sum total of its predicates and, therefore, to deny that the substance has any one of those predicates is a contradiction. For instance, it is a contradiction to deny that Eve tasted the apple. Thus, it seems that all truths are necessary and that none of them is contingent.

Nevertheless, Leibniz does distinguish between necessary and contingent truths. He deals with this point in section 13 of the *Discourse on Metaphysics*. The theory of truth is an account of what it is for a predicate to be truly attributed to a subject, but this does not mean that the subject actually exists. So, although it is a contradiction to deny that Eve tasted the apple, we can deny without contradiction that Eve ever existed. Propositions that assert actual existence are contingent, or only hypothetically necessary, rather than absolutely necessary. The one exception to this claim is the proposition that God exists, which is not contingent, but is absolutely necessary.

We can explain the point also as follows. This actual world is only one among many possible worlds. Possible worlds are individuated by contingent facts: if any contingent fact were different, then we would inhabit a different possible world. However, logically necessary truths are true in all possible worlds. For example, the proposition '2+2 = 4' is a necessary proposition; that is, it is true in all possible worlds. God freely chooses which of all possible worlds to make actual and this choice is the source of contingency in Leibniz's system. He calls this 'the principle of contingency or of the existence of things'. God chooses what should exist.

According to the definition of truth in which the subject–concept contains the predicate–concept, propositions such as 'Eve tasted the apple' are reducible to identical propositions. For this reason, such propositions are necessary truths and are true in all possible worlds. This claim requires a special analysis of singular propositions, such as 'Eve tasted the apple.' Normally we take such propositions to have existential import; that is we say that 'Eve tasted the apple' is true if and only if there actually existed a person, Eve, who in fact ate the apple. However, Leibniz claims that such singular propositions do not have existential import: their truth does not depend upon the existence of individuals. The proposition is true even if Eve never existed. In this way, it is similar to propositions such as 'all unicorns are animals' or 'all triangles have three sides.' Such statements merely assert that certain concepts include other concepts, and, therefore, their truth does not depend on the existence of individuals. These propositions are true, even if no triangles or unicorns actually exist.

In summary, singular proposition (such as 'Eve tasted the apple') and universal propositions (such as 'all triangles have three sides') are necessary truths, but they have no existential import. Their truth does not depend on the existence of individuals. On the other hand, the existence of any individuals, e.g. of a triangle, of Eve, of Adam, is a contingent fact, and depends on the free choice of God.

The internal nature of any individual substance is fixed logically, although it is a contingent matter whether that individual substance exists. The one exception is God who must exist. In brief, Leibniz claims that all existential propositions, except those asserting the existence of God, are contingent and, furthermore, that only existential propositions are contingent.

Implications

Leibniz's distinction between necessary and contingent truths has important ramifications for the Principle of Sufficient Reason. As we have already mentioned, this principle states that everything must have a cause or sufficient reason. This is equivalent to the requirement that there should be an a priori proof of every proposition. However, the proofs of contingent and necessary propositions are different.

Necessary propositions are those whose denial is a contradiction or, as Leibniz puts it, their opposite involves a contradiction. These propositions are true in all possible worlds. They are either explicitly analytic, such as 'every circle is a circle', or they can be reduced to an explicitly analytic proposition by a finite process of analysis. Analysis is the breaking down of any complex idea into its constituent parts. Ultimately, these constituent parts will be the simple ideas or primitive concepts, the 'alphabet of human thought'. In summary, all necessary truths have to be provable a priori, for they are either explicitly analytic or can be made explicitly analytic by a finite process of analysis.

However, contingent existential propositions are provable a priori but, in their case, the proof will be infinitely long. This is the crucial difference between the necessary and the contingent: the a priori proof of contingent existential propositions is infinitely long and involves a reference to the free will of God. This is because contingency in the world is due to the free will of God, for God chooses what exists.

Why is the proof of any contingent proposition infinitely long? Leibniz argues that we can know a priori that God exists, and furthermore, that God chooses the best of all possible worlds. Thus we can know a priori that the actual world is the best of all possible worlds. This means that to show that there is sufficient reason for any contingent fact, we have to demonstrate that the fact is part of the best of all possible worlds. In other words, to give proof of any contingent fact involves showing how the fact is a part of a causal chain that forms the best of all possible worlds. This is an infinitely long proof.

Any contingent existential fact can be deduced from an earlier state of the universe, given the laws of nature. Since we know a priori that God chooses the best, the laws of nature he chooses will be for the best. For example, the laws will be such as to realize the greatest variety of form with the least effort (see chapter 9). In this way, the principle of the best can provide us with some limited a priori knowledge of the world. However, the complete infinite proof of any contingent fact can be known only to God, because it involves comparing an infinity of possible worlds. For this reason, Leibniz compares the contingent to the resolution of a surd, such as the square root of 2, which is an infinitely long decimal, while he compares the necessary to an integer that can be analyzed into a finite number of prime factors. Because the a priori proofs of contingent propositions are infinitely long, humans have to learn these facts a posteriori, by experience.

Relations

Let us return to the first part of Leibniz's theory of the proposition: that all propositions can be reduced to the subject-predicate form. Among the most important propositions not of the subject–predicate form are relational propositions, such as 'Jesus was the son of Mary', or 'A is longer than B'. Propositions of this type seem to have two subjects and they suggest that there is a complex fact such that a certain relation holds between those two subjects. Relational propositions do not assert that a property belongs to a substance but, according to Leibniz, they must be reducible to such an assertion.

In his fifth paper to Clarke, Leibniz sets out three ways of conceiving the relation of length between two lines L and M:

a) as the ratio of L to M,
b) as the ratio of M to L and,
c) as a ratio between L and M abstracted from both lines.

Leibniz considers this last way of conceiving relations mistaken. It cannot be affirmed of both L and M together that they are the subject of this relation; for instance, if L is twice as long as M, it cannot be asserted that both L and M are the subjects of the ratio two to one. A ratio and relation considered in this way is a "mere ideal thing" or it is an "entity of reason." This means that a ratio of two to one is not a real thing, but rather a mental construction, which has its basis in the non-relational properties of substance.

Leibniz affirms: "There are no purely extrinsic denominations." This means that relations are reducible to the properties of substances, and that when a proposition expressed by a relational sentence is true, it is true by virtue of the truth of some subject–predicate propositions. In other words, relational propositions can be reduced to purely subject–predicate propositions. If we claim that A has relation R to B, the same thing can be affirmed by asserting that A has certain properties and that B has certain properties. Parkinson calls this Leibniz's weaker thesis about relations (Parkinson, 1985).

Leibniz also argues for a stronger thesis about the nature of relations: if substance A has relation R to B, then this can be reduced to subject–predicate propositions about A alone or to subject–predicate propositions about B alone. This stronger thesis is important for the theory of monads, which we shall examine in chapter 8.

To appreciate Leibniz's reductive analysis of relations, we must distinguish between a symmetrical and asymmetrical relation. 'Is similar to' stands for a symmetrical relation, because if A is similar to B then B is similar to A. Leibniz holds that the proposition 'A is similar to B' can be reduced to the two subject–predicate propositions 'A has property F now' and 'B has property F now'. Concerning asymmetrical relations, he claims the proposition 'Paris is the lover of Helen' can be reduced to the proposition 'Paris loves and by that very fact Helen is loved.'

5
The Labyrinth of Physics

The seventeenth century was a very exciting time in the study of physics, a new science which was just being conceived. At the beginning of the century, physical changes tended to be explained in superstitious terms. The typical characteristics of bodies were often explained as an expression of their innate tendencies. For example, it is the innate nature of things made of earth to fall; for things made of fire to rise. Everything is composed of at least one of the four elements: earth, water, air and fire.

During the seventeenth century, this medieval view of matter was replaced slowly by a mechanical view, according to which there is only one kind of matter in terms of which all physical appearances, such as colors, can be explained. Furthermore, the new physics held up the prospect that all physical changes can be explained in terms of a few mechanical and mathematically expressible laws.

Leibniz was an important theoretical physicist of the late 17th century. The major aspects of his philosophy of physics are:

1) The rejection of Descartes' physics
2) The rejection of atomism and Newton's theory of gravity
3) His own positive theory of forces and matter
4) His work on the calculus
5) The theory of space and time, which opposes Newton's

Leibniz rejects both of the two important physical theories of his day: Descartes' and Newton's (1 and 2 above). He challenges Descartes' view of matter, but also argues vigorously against the atomistic view of matter. He replaces them with his own theory (3) above), which is a portal to his metaphysics. This three-way discussion will be the main focus of this chapter. His work on the calculus, the fourth item on the list, will be examined in the appendix to this chapter. The theory of space and time, the fifth item above, will be the theme of the next chapter.

Rejection of Descartes

Descartes' theory of physics was dominant in Europe until around 1680. In the 1630's, Descartes had not only articulated many basic principles of modern science, but had also effectively laid down a program for the development of physics. This program is based on his idea that all the properties of matter are geometrical. Descartes tries to show how all purely physical changes can be explained mechanically solely in terms of the spatial properties of objects: shape, size, position and motion. He argues that the essence of matter is spatial extension and, furthermore, that all of a body's properties are modes of spatial extension.

Against this, Leibniz argues that extension cannot constitute the sole essence of a body. Matter must have some non-geometrical properties. It cannot consist of merely being extended, because there must be something to be extended, or simultaneously and continuously repeated. According to Leibniz, the non-geometrical property of matter, which fills out space by being continuously repeated, is the force of resistance. In other words, whereas Descartes asserts that extension is the fundamental feature of matter, Leibniz contends the contrary: that the essence of matter consists in forces of resistance and not in spatial extension, and that extension itself arises because the forces of resistance are repeated in a continuous way.

Second, whereas according to Descartes spatial extension is simple or unanalyzable, Leibniz contends that extension is analyzable in terms of plurality, continuity and co-existence. Spatial extension consists of a continuous repeating of that which is co-existent. For this reason, extension cannot constitute the essence of matter.

In the 1698 paper, *On Nature Itself*, Leibniz argues that Descartes' ontology would make change impossible. Descartes' definition of matter as extension means that the universe is full of a uniform matter. Under this assumption of uniformity, it makes no sense to distinguish one part of matter from another and thus, the very idea of motion becomes impossible. It becomes impossible to affirm that particular pieces of matter have moved, because there is nothing that distinguishes them from any others. Furthermore, Descartes' view of matter prevents him from formulating correctly a principle of conservation, as we shall now see.

Dynamics

In 1686, Leibniz published an important article, called *Brevis Demonstratio Erroris Memorabilis Cartesii*, in which he argued that Descartes' principle of the conservation of motion is false. This leads Leibniz to make important distinctions among the concepts of physics. First, Descartes does not distinguish between motion and velocity. Velocity is the measure of the distance covered in a specific direction in a particular time. Velocity is essentially directional; motion is not.

Second, Descartes' principle ignores the idea of mass. Therefore, it cannot "relate the fast motion of a small body to the slow motion of a large one." (Ross, p38). If Descartes' position were true, then it would follow that

> upon contact, the smallest body would impart its speed to the largest body without losing any of its speed. (*Discourse*, 21)

Consequently, Descartes' rules of motion "violate the equality of cause and effect." Leibniz claims that the cause and effect must be equal and that Descartes' laws of motion contradict this equality.

This might lead one to conclude that Leibniz thinks that momentum, or velocity times mass, is conserved rather than Descartes' cruder notion of motion. However, from 1678, Leibniz argues that what actually is conserved is a live force or energy, which he calls *vis viva*, and which he argues is identical to mass times velocity squared or mv^2. This is because the velocity of a falling body is proportional to the square root of the distance it travels. In other words, the distance a falling body travels is proportional to its velocity squared. Consequently, it is *vis viva* or live force that is conserved in the collision between two bodies. For Leibniz, the concept of live force is vital. Indeed he envisages a science of power or dynamics to replace Newton's kinematics, the science of motion.

Gravity and Matter

Although Descartes' physics was widely accepted and taught in universities throughout Europe by the 1660's, the publication in 1687 of Newton's *Principia* meant the gradual replacement of Cartesian physics by the more comprehensive Newtonian system.

One of the essential ideas of the mechanistic view of nature is that all changes in one physical body must be transmitted through some physical mechanism to another. However, Newton's theory of gravity apparently constitutes a violation of this idea, because Newton portrays gravity as a genuine action at a distance. According to this, a body can affect other distant bodies without some intervening mechanism.

Leibniz thinks that all physical changes can be explained mechanically. He rejects Newton's notion of gravity, calling it a miraculous force. Furthermore, Newton treats gravity as an entity apart from bodies and their motion, when he has no right to. In other words, Newton treats mass and velocity as real and defines 'force' in terms of them. Consequently, in the Newtonian system, force should be nothing apart from mass and velocity. Therefore, in Newton's system, force cannot explain changes in velocity and cannot be treated as something independent.

In 1689 Leibniz published an article, *Essay Concerning the Causes of the Motions of the Heavenly Bodies*, in which he attempts to give an explanation of the movement of the planets which is thoroughly mechanistic, i.e. without relying on the occult force of gravity. He notes that the planets rotate in the same direction and nearly in the same plane. He tries to explain in detail their movement in terms of vortices or the circulation of fluids around the sun which have a velocity inversely proportional to their distance from the center (i.e. the sun). By taking into account centrifugal forces and the gravitational attraction of the sun working through the fluids, Leibniz also tries to reconcile the vortices with Newton's mathematics.

Atoms

According to Leibniz, the atomist position cannot explain cohesion, or how a collection of atoms constitutes a single body. If only atoms exist, then the atomist cannot appeal to a distinctive cohesive force to explain how atoms cohere. In this way, the idea of a cohesive force is no better than that of gravity.

Some thinkers explain this phenomenon by claiming that atoms had something akin to hooks and eyes to hold them together. However, this merely repeats the problem. If atoms have different parts, then there must be some explanation of how the parts cohere together. Obviously, this kind of solution reproduces the problem ad infinitum. Furthermore, if atoms have different shapes, then they have distinguishable parts and they would not really be atoms. This argument presupposes that atoms must be defined as intrinsically indivisible, and this is an important point for Leibniz, to which we will return later.

Leibniz rejects the very notion of a physical atom, because all matter is infinitely divisible. A non-divisible atom would have to be a body of perfect hardness. Such bodies would have no flexibility. Consequently, in any collision they would instantly change direction. This, according to Leibniz, would be a violation of the principle of continuity. There can be no instantaneous reactions, because real collisions always take time. The bodies involved always have a size, and they are neither infinitely hard nor elastic. Consequently, it takes time for the first body to squash the second and for the first to slow down as the second accelerates. Such is the mechanism by which forces are transferred.

This is one of the criticisms that Leibniz makes of Newton's physics: Newton treats particles as if they were both infinitely hard and infinitely elastic, capable of transmitting force instantaneously. He also treats them as if they had a location at a point i.e. as if they had no size. Furthermore, Newton connects particles by forces that operate at a distance. In short, Newton's physics is idealized, and could not be true of the real physical world. (Newton was aware of these problems but he saw these abstractions as necessary to describe reality mathematically).

The New Alternative

We have seen that Leibniz rejects the Cartesian claim that the essence of matter is extension. According to Leibniz, there must be something to be extended, namely something with mass. On the other hand, Leibniz also repudiates the alternative position: that matter consists in indivisible atoms in space.

What is Leibniz's alternative? It consists of two parts. First, in the paper *Specimen Dynamicum*, published in 1695, he introduces an ontology of forces. In so doing he rejects the assumption that matter is inert. Secondly, he tries to solve the problem of the continuum.

The Theory of Forces

Leibniz postulates the existence of two basic kinds of force: passive and active. The active force is connected to motion and acceleration, and the passive force to the capacity of things to resist, for example, to impenetrability.

This passive force or resistance constitutes the extension of a body in space. In other words, extension is the power of bodies to resist others. This claim abandons the traditional notion of matter: the very idea of matter as nothing more than a passive host for forces makes little sense; its only role is to satisfy the assumption that forces must inhere in something. Leibniz concludes that prime matter is only the capacity to resist other bodies. In contemporary terms, one might say that he reduces matter to pure energy.

Leibniz's view is that material things consist in the union of the two primitive forces, the active and passive. In *On Nature Itself* (1698), he writes:

> The very substance of things consists in a force for acting and being acted upon (Loemker, p. 502).

Furthermore, Leibniz argues that the two forces are related to one another as form and matter: the form is the active force and the matter the passive resisting force. In this way, he resurrects the Aristotelian distinction between form and matter, and argues for a conception of matter that treats material particles as fields of force or point-like particles of energy.

Leibniz claims that the primitive forces which make up material bodies give rise to derivative forces when two bodies interact. These derivative forces are what we measure in collisions or physical interactions and are the subject matter of physics. These derivative forces are modifications or limitations of the primary forces.

Because Leibniz's approach to nature is mechanistic, the basic physical interaction is the collision of two "particles." This applies not only to the interaction between two separate physical objects, such as two billiard balls, but also to all of the parts and sub-parts of the balls themselves as they collide. In other words, just as one billiard ball moves the other by pushing it, so too with all the parts of the two balls. The problem is that this process of pushing and compressing of parts applies to smaller and smaller parts on to infinity. No matter how small the parcels of matter, there can be no direct transfer of force. Such a transfer would be open to the same objections as Newton's mysterious notion of gravity. Because of this infinite regress, Leibniz concludes that strictly speaking forces cannot be transferred at all. He expresses this by claiming that all action is spontaneous.

The Labyrinth of the Continuum

35

The second part of Leibniz's alternative to Descartes' and Newton's physics is his solution to the problem of the continuum. Leibniz coins the phrase 'the labyrinth of the composition of the continuum', to refer to the problem of how things in the world can be composed out of a continuum. Anything in space is infinitely divisible because space does not consist of discrete units, but rather is a continuum.

As we have seen, Descartes thinks of matter as being the same as spatial extension. Therefore, for him, matter is essentially continuous. However, this view makes it impossible to explain how a infinite continuous blob of space-matter could manifest itself as solids, liquids and gases, without appeal to the notion of mass. Descartes tried to do this by postulating three different kinds of corpuscles on the basis of differences in their movements. However, Leibniz objects that there must be something over and above space itself to move. Descartes takes the idea of the continuum seriously, but he cannot explain how material things are constituted. On the other hand, atomists take the idea of an atomic unit seriously, but cannot explain how such a thing can exist in a continuum. Genuine atoms should be indivisible, but, argues Leibniz, anything that exists in space is infinitely divisible.

The solution seems to be to assume that the only genuine atoms are mathematical dimensionless points. Indeed, Leibniz's solution to this problem is to affirm that matter consists of dimensionless points of force in constant motion. He argues that every piece of three dimensional matter is composed of an infinity of points of force in constant motion.

However, this claim on its own does not explain how material objects exist, because such atoms are dimensionless. How could three dimensional material things be built out of dimensionless points of force? Leibniz answer to this question is strikingly simple. He argues that matter and space are derivative existents. We might express this dramatically by claiming that, for Leibniz, space and material objects are merely appearances: reality consists of an infinity of dimensionless points of force or monads.

More accurately, in his letters to Arnauld in 1686/7, Leibniz argues that matter cannot be a substance. All substances must be simple and indivisible. Things that are aggregates depend for their reality on their parts and, because of this dependence, no substance can be an aggregate. However, as everything in space is infinitely divisible, something extended cannot be a substance at all. The only substances in the created world are monads. We will examine Leibniz's theory of monads in chapter 8.

Furthermore, as we have seen, Leibniz claims that spatial extension is the continuous repeating of the passive force of resistance or impenetrability. In other words, Leibniz solves the problem of the continuum by arguing that matter continuously extended in space is only a derivative existent.

Conclusion

Leibniz's arguments against both Cartesian and atomistic physics lead him to positive conclusions about the nature of matter and space which are important steps towards his metaphysics. First, matter consists in certain living forces. Second, despite the fact that physical changes appear mechanical, these forces act spontaneously. Third, the substances that constitute reality cannot exist in space. These three points indicate that reality is very different from what it seems.

Appendix: Mathematics

The Calculus

In the first edition of the *Principia Mathematica* of 1687, Newton wrote:

> In letters which went between me and that most excellent geometrer, G.W.Leibniz ten years ago, when I signified that I was in a method of determining maxima and minima, of drawing tangents and the like, that most distinguished man wrote back that he had also fallen upon a method of the same kind, and communicated his method which hardly differed from mine except in forms of words and symbols

Who discovered the calculus first? Newton had developed the method in 1664, though he had not published anything. In 1669 Newton communicated his method of fluxions to his friends by letter but it was only in 1704 that he published his *New Method*.

Leibniz discovered the calculus in October 1675. In September 1684, he expounded the differential calculus in a published paper and in 1686, he published a paper explaining the integral calculus. Therefore, it seems clear that Newton discovered the calculus first, and that Leibniz encountered it independently. Additionally, the notation we use today for both integration and differentiation comes from Leibniz.

However, during their lifetimes and beyond, there was a forceful priority dispute concerning the calculus between Leibniz and Newton and their respective supporters. This dispute originated in the fact that, on his visit to London in 1673, Leibniz met Oldenburg, the secretary of the Royal Society, who knew of Newton's work. Later, some of Newton's friends suggested that, during this visit, Leibniz received an explanation of Newton's method. Furthermore, in June 1676, Newton wrote to Leibniz explaining some of his mathematical results. In August, Leibniz replied to Oldenburg with a letter explaining his own work in calculus. However, it is clear from the text of Newton's letter that Leibniz could not have learned the method of the calculus from this source.

In 1699, a Swiss mathematician suggested to the Royal Society that Leibniz had borrowed his calculus from Newton. In reply, in 1705, Leibniz wrote an anonymous review of Newton's *Optics* in which he suggested that Newton had borrowed Leibniz's own calculus. In 1712, the Royal Society appointed an investigative committee to examine the documents involved. It ruled that Newton had made the discovery first, but left open the question as to whether Leibniz had independently discovered the calculus. In 1716, Leibniz protested that Newton's original acknowledgment, quoted above, should have settled the question of his own independent discovery of the calculus. This kind of dispute was almost inevitable given the nature of research of the times. This was the age of individual geniuses who vied with one another across the whole continent of Europe. Newton himself postponed the publication of his *Optics* until after the death of Hooker to avoid a priority dispute.

Mathematics

Leibniz did much of his primary mathematical work in Paris (1672-76). He discovered the basic principles of topology, calling it analysis situs, which later became important for the development of non-Euclidean geometries (p.29, Ross). During this period, Leibniz also "discovered" binary arithmetic and he worked on the geometry of infinitesimals.

The infinitesimal calculus consists of two parts: differentiation and integration. Differentiation allows one to calculate the rate of change at any moment of a quantity which is a function of another. Integration permits the calculation of a whole from a given value at any moment; for example, the area under a curve.

In Paris, Leibniz was concerned with the ancient problem of how to square the circle, which means how to construct a square with exactly the same area as a given circle. Since the area of a circle is πr^2, part of this involved finding an exact numerical value for π. Leibniz made an apparently important step towards this when he discovered that $\pi/4 = 1/1 - 1/3 + 1/5 - 1/7 + ...$ This encouraged Leibniz to work on the problem of how to sum an infinite series. In turn, this led him to the idea of an infinite series that converges on a limit. The differential calculus was a method for calculating the limit of such a series and integration for determining the sum. Leibniz's work on the calculus went in tandem with his thinking about the problem of the continuum. In turn, this influenced his thinking on space, time and the nature of reality itself.

6
Space and Time

In the last year of his life, 1716, Leibniz expounded his theory of space and time in his letters to Clarke. In these letters, he advocates a relational theory of space and time, directly opposed to the Newtonian absolute theory put forward by Clarke. These letters have become a philosophical classic.

According to the Newtonian theory, space is logically prior to the matter which may or may not occupy it. Space is an unlimited whole and any region of space is a part of the one unlimited infinite whole. Bodies occupy parts of space and, although bodies have volume, space is not a property of bodies. Because the absolute theory affirms that space is prior to the bodies that happen to occupy it, the theory entails that it is meaningful to suppose that a finite, material universe could have been differently situated in absolute, infinite space. For example, the collection of all material bodies could have been situated 10 meters to the left of where it actually is located. Their position could have been different in relation to absolute space. Thus, for Newton's theory, it is meaningful to suppose that the whole finite material universe might move with respect to absolute space. Similar statements apply to time and, more specifically, the universe could have been created earlier or later than it in fact was with respect to absolute time. Consequently, according to Newton's theory, absolute motion is possible. It is motion with respect to absolute space for a period of absolute time.

The Rejection of Absolute Space

Leibniz's own theory of space and time has two aspects. First, in contrast to Newton, he denies the existence of absolute space and time. Space is not a container which exists logically prior to and independent of physical bodies. He claims that the existence of matter is logically prior to the existence of space: physical objects or forces happen to be ordered spatially and space is nothing over and above these spatial relations. It is merely a system of relations.

This relational view of space has several consequences. First, it implies that it is meaningless to suggest that the universe could have been created in a different position and can change position in space. There is no absolute space and an object can change position only relative to another object. It cannot change position in relation to absolute space. Space is nothing over and above the spatial relations between objects and, consequently, it is meaningless to suppose that all objects could have been differently situated. Similarly for time: according to the relational theory, it is meaningless to suppose that the universe could have been created earlier or later, because time is nothing over and above the temporal relations between events. There is no absolute time. God creates time by creating temporally related events. There can be no time before the creation of events.

Because he rejects the concepts of absolute space and time, Leibniz also rejects the idea of absolute motion. There can be no such thing as motion against the background of unmoving absolute space. The motion of any physical body must be relative to the motion of other physical bodies. In 1689, he writes:

> Motion in all mathematical rigor is nothing but a change in the positions of bodies with respect to one another, and so motion is not something absolute but consists in a relation (AG91).

This leads to a second implication of the relational theory. The theory implies that there can be no vacuum or void. Leibniz denies the existence of empty space, not because he thinks space must be full, but because he rejects the very idea of space as a container, the parts of which can be full or empty. The concept of a vacuum should be rejected because it presupposes the idea that space is absolute.

Leibniz's Arguments

Leibniz argues for the relational theory by claiming that Newton's view contravenes the Principle of Sufficient Reason. He says that God could have no possible reason for creating the universe in a different region of space or at a different period of time. Since everything must have a sufficient reason, it cannot make sense to say that the universe could have been created earlier or elsewhere in space; these cannot be genuine alternatives, contrary to the claims of the absolute theory. Therefore, the theory is false.

Furthermore, Newton's theory is a violation of the Principle of the Identity of Indiscernibles. Points and empty regions of absolute space are clearly qualitatively similar in all respects (i.e. they are indiscernible), and yet the absolute theory maintains that they are numerically distinct.

Leibniz also challenges Newton's view on theological grounds. The Newtonian idea of space and time as absolute, infinite entities contradicts the uniqueness of God. If God is the only infinite individual, space and time cannot be absolute and infinite.

Newton has an argument in favor of his own theory. He claims that we can distinguish relative from absolute motion, that is motion with respect to absolute space. Newton's assertion was based on the hypothetical experiment of a bucket full of water revolving in space. In such a case, the water would climb up the sides of the bucket. According to Newton, this shows that it is the bucket that is revolving and not the rest of the universe. In other words, this would count as an example of absolute motion.

Leibniz's argument against Newton is ingenious. He points out that Newton's reasoning depends on the distinction between movement in a curve (curvilinear motion) and movement in a straight line (rectilinear motion). Newton admits that there are no possible experimental grounds for distinguishing between relative and absolute movement in the case of rectilinear motion. Leibniz uses this point to argue against Newton. He claims that the distinction between curvilinear and rectilinear movement cannot be used to establish the existence of absolute motion, because all curvilinear movement is made up of tiny segments of rectilinear motion. In this way, Leibniz defends the claim that motion considered strictly as a change of place or position is relative. There is no way of affirming whether it is A that moves with respect to B, or vice versa.

An argument for forces

The relativity of motion is an important conclusion because it indicates the need for an ontology of forces. His reasoning for this point is as follows. Suppose that A and B are moving relative to each other. The relativity of motion implies that, without some further consideration, we cannot affirm whether it is A moving with respect to B or vice versa. This entails that we cannot affirm that the motion is a property of A, nor that it is a property of B. However, if it is real, the motion must be the property of something. It cannot be merely or purely relational. For, as we saw in chapter four, all relations must be reducible to the properties of some substance. Consequently, if motion is real, then it must be grounded in something apart from mere changes in relative position. This something else is force.

According to Leibniz, force is non-arbitrary. For example, if A and B are moving relative to each other, then at least one of the bodies must have been endowed with a positive force that caused the motion. In other words, active force is not purely relative; the cause of the motion must have belonged to some determinate body.

In summary, when we consider motion as merely the changing of relative position, it is utterly arbitrary whether A or B moves. However, there is more to motion than changes in position, because the reality of motion must be grounded in forces, which are absolute.

The Unreality of Space and Time

As we saw in the previous chapter, Leibniz argues that reality consists only of substances and their properties, and that these substances are non-spatially extended monads. These claims have the dramatic implication that material objects in space are not fundamentally real. Now, given this theory of space and time, Leibniz can offer a different argument for the same conclusion. As we have seen in chapter 4, he argues that relations are ideal, i.e.. not real. This point, together with the relational theory of space and time, implies that space and time are unreal or ideal. In other words,

1. All relations are ideal
2. Space and time are nothing but relations

   _____

3. Therefore, space and time are ideal

This argument supports the contention that reality consists of non-spatial monads. This contention is the basis of Leibniz's positive explanation of what space and time are. Space and time are appearances which have their real basis in the points of view of monads.

Conclusions

We can draw some interim conclusions about the nature of reality based on what we have learned so far of Leibniz's overall philosophy.

First, one of the fundamental bases of his thinking is that substance must be a true unit. As we saw in chapter five, this implies that substances must be indivisible and, therefore, they cannot have spatial extension. In this way, they are non-spatial and, initially, it is best to conceive them as dimensionless points.

Second, in this chapter, we have seen that Leibniz holds a relational view of space and time. Space and time are not substance-like. They are merely relations, and all relational statements are reducible to subject-predicate propositions. This has the important implication that space and time are not fundamentally real. These first two points indicate why matter is something unreal.

Third, for reasons we also saw in chapter five, substance as something essentially active. It consists of, or gives rise to, certain forces. Motion can be explained only given this supposition. Consequently, these dimensionless point-like substances can be conceived provisionally as points of activity or energy.

Fourth, as we saw in chapter four, every substance must have a complete concept. In this way, each substance is like a universe unto itself that develops according to its own concept or nature.

Now we are ready to turn to Leibniz's theory of biology and psychology to understand better his view of substance.

7

Mind and Cause

Can the mechanistic approach to nature be applied to human actions and consciousness? Mechanists explain changes in terms of some physical process which follows a deterministic law. In doing so, they deny that the relevant phenomena can be explained as a goal-directed action, or in terms of some purpose. In this way, they should be contrasted with vitalists, who explain phenomena in terms of purposes and thoughts. The debate between mechanism versus vitalism is of great importance to the philosophy of Leibniz. It marks the transition from physics to metaphysics. The gateway is the notion of living force.

The Limits of Mechanism

Are we machines? Descartes (1596-1650) answers no. He draws a sharp distinction between the mind and the body and argues that while material is always mechanical, the mind is not. In effect, Descartes places the mind outside nature.

In contrast, Leibniz's answer to this question has two layers. On the level of phenomena, or of material things, Leibniz is a mechanist. He thinks that all physical changes must be explained in mechanical terms. Indeed, this is the basis of his arguments against Newton's notion of gravity: it is not a mechanical explanation.

However, as we have seen, the whole mechanical, spatial and material universe is only derivative or secondary. A proper explanation of motion and space reveals that the true nature of reality is entirely different. It consists in indivisible, dimensionless substances, or

45

monads. Consequently, mechanism is only an abstraction from a deeper reality that should be expressed in terms of spontaneous development and purpose. In other words, nature can be explained mechanistically, but the deeper reality is quite different: it is organic and vital.

Why does Leibniz think this? First, there is the problem of the transmission of force (cf. Ch.3). When one object collides with another, the outer particles of the first body must push those of the second, but since anything in space is a compound, this process must be true of the parts of these particles, and of the parts of those parts, and so on to infinity. Given this infinite regress, forces cannot be transmitted at all. Substances change spontaneously, because of their internal nature, rather than because of external causes.

Second, this result is reinforced by Leibniz's philosophy of language. He defines substance as a self-sufficient entity. As we saw in chapter 4, the concept of each individual substance must be complete in order that each substance can be distinguished in principle from all other possible substances. This completeness requires that the subject is characterized by all the predicates true of it. Furthermore, his definition of truth as containment means that all those truths are analytic. The upshot is that each substance is entirely determined by its own nature or complete concept.

However, there is another important ingredient. Leibniz writes:

> when I tried to get to the bottom of the actual principles of mechanics..., I became aware that the consideration of an extended mass is not of itself enough and that use must also be made of the notion of force (p170, Brown).

The notion of living force, which is required to explain motion, is a point of transition from the physical to the metaphysical. Because matter really consists of such forces, the universe consists of substances that should be thought of as active, as having purposes, as we shall now see.

Substantial points

Nothing made of parts can be a substance. Everything in space is made of parts. Thus nothing in space is a substance. In the draft of a letter to Arnauld, Leibniz writes:

> The substance of a body, if it has one, must be indivisible;
> whether we call it soul or form is indifferent to me (p140
> Brown)

He takes the self or soul as the paradigmatic model of substantial unity. This means that all substances can be conceived by analogy with the soul. Let us see why.

Differences of Degree

From about 1687, Leibniz used what he called the principle of continuity in his thinking:

> the nature of things is uniform, and our nature cannot differ
> infinitely from the other simple substances of which the
> universe consists (p.171, Brown)

Of course, this does not deny that there are enormous differences between a human and, for instance, a stone. It means that there are no gaps or radical differences of kind in nature; there are only gradual differences of degree. "Nature makes no leaps."

At times this vision of a continual chain of being sounds almost evolutionist. Leibniz writes that humans:

> are linked with animals, these with plants, and these again
> with fossils, which in turn are connected with those bodies
> which sense and imagination represent to us as dead and
> inorganic (Letter to Guhrauer, p. 676, Durant).

Now, we can list the reasons why substances, or monads, are analogous with the soul. There are four points. First, nature consists of active forces. This means rejecting the conception of matter as something dead and inert. It implies that we should conceive of substance as having something akin to appetite or desire. It does not mean that all substances literally have desires, but rather that they have an "internal principle" of change (*Monodology*, 15).

Second, as we shall see later, each substance expresses the whole universe. This does not mean that each substance literally has conscious perceptions of the universe. Leibniz affirms that an algebraic equation can express a circle, without resembling it. Nevertheless, it does mean that each substance has something analogous with sense.

47

Third, true substances or monads are not extended in space. In this respect, they are more similar to the soul than to material bodies. Being non-spatial, they are non-material, and in this way they are like souls. Given that all substances must be indivisible, and given that extended matter cannot be a substance, it is easy to see why substances must be mind–like entities with mental states. If they are not extended, what else could they be? If the only candidate attributes are extension and consciousness, and if extension cannot be an attribute of substances, then the only option is consciousness. Furthermore, if reality only appears to be extended, then it must appear so to some mind. This points to the primacy of the perceiving mind. Moreover, according to Leibniz, souls are paradigms of unity. By definition, all substances must be a unity; the soul clearly is such unity. In this respect, all substances are comparable to souls.

Finally, there is the principle of continuity mentioned above. All other substances that are not souls must be like souls, because of the principle of continuity. For these reasons, Leibniz concludes that all monads, even those that constitute what we would consider to be dead, inanimate things, are like souls. He writes:

> I believe rather that everything is full of animate bodies and to my mind there are incomparably more souls than there are atoms.. (p. 294, ed. Jolley)

Psychological Implications

The claim that the universe consists of an infinity of substances that are all to varying degrees like souls has interesting implications for psychology. It means that the differences between humans and the other animals is one of degree. It has the same implication for the differences between living and non-living things.

Leibniz agrees with Descartes and Locke that the difference between humans and other animals is that only humans possess both consciousness and reason. However, Leibniz thinks that the factors that cause our behavior are usually unconscious and, in this respect, we are more similar to the other animals than we might think. Furthermore, Leibniz believes that there are unconscious mental states. In arguing this, he opposes the standard view of his time, which held that we are necessarily aware of our own mental states. We should distinguish between perception, which consists of conscious mental states, and apperception, which consists in being aware of a perception. In other words, being conscious does not require awareness that one is conscious. Furthermore, Leibniz argues that any perception is composed of many tiny perceptions of which one is not aware (see Ch.12).

Back to Mechanism

Ultimately the universe consists in an infinity of mind-like substances called monads. At this level, changes should be explained in vitalistic terms, using the notion of purpose. Nevertheless, at the physical level, which is derivative or secondary, changes should be explained mechanistically.

Our original question was: How can beings who have purposes exist in a mechanistic universe? Leibniz answer this question by accepting both mechanism and vitalism. He combines them by distinguishing two levels. He writes:

> In general, we must hold that everything in the world can be explained in two ways: through ...efficient causes and through final causes (p.327 ed. Jolley).

This answer opens the door to many new questions concerning, for example, the nature of monads and their relation to the appearance of matter; these will be clarified in the next chapter. For the moment, we can note that Leibniz's theory requires that there is a perfect harmony between the two types of explanation. In the *Monadology* he writes:

> We established a perfect harmony between two natural kingdoms, the one of efficient causes and the other of final causes (# 87)

How does he establish this?

Causation

Descartes postulated the existence of two radically different kinds of substance: mind and matter. At the same time he argued that they must be in a close causal union. The mind and the body must causally influence each other.

This causal dualism is problematic. How can two substances so different from each other, causally affect each other? Remember that, according to Descartes, the sole essence of the mind is to be conscious and the sole essence of matter is to be in space. Given this, the postulated causal relations between them appears to be magical and quite contrary to the mechanistic explanations of nature. Many philosophers of the next generation, such as Spinoza (1632-1677) and Malbranche (1638-1715), denied this causation.

Leibniz accepts the principle that two unlike substances cannot causally interact. In 1695, in the *New System* he writes:

> For I can find no way of explaining how the body causes something to happen in the soul, nor vice versa, nor how one created substance can communicate with another (§12).

As we shall see, the sting is in the tail of this sentence: Leibniz argues that there is no causation at all between finite substances, even of the same kind. Of course, it appears that changes in one substance can cause changes in another. This, however, is due to a pre-established harmony in creation. Monads are like a series of clocks that keep time together without being actually connected. What keeps the monads running in a pre-established harmony is that each has its content predetermined by its complete concept.

There are two lines of argument that lead to this conclusion. First, individual substances do not causally interact because they are completely spontaneous in their changes. All changes come from within, or rather from an internal principle. This is so because everything that is true of a substance can be deduced from its individual nature or complete concept. In other words, Leibniz's doctrine of pre-established harmony has its roots in the assertion that each substance must have a complete concept and in the theory of truth as concept inclusion (see sections §8-9 of the *New System*). Each substance develops spontaneously from its own complete nature. Because of this, there is no possibility of any causal relations between substances, and because of this, appearances are best explained in terms of a pre-established harmony.

Second, by definition, a substance is self-sufficient: otherwise it would dependent on something else, which is contrary to the nature of substances. It is for this reason that a smile is not a substance: the existence of a smile depends on a smiling person. Leibniz understands the self-sufficiency of substance to imply that the characteristics of each substance must depend only on the substance itself. This in turn implies that no substance can depend on another for its nature, which effectively rules out the possibility of causation between substances.

8
Monads

What does reality consist of? We now have gathered all the elements from the many aspects of Leibniz's philosophy to explain his theory of monads. It remains only to pull them together to understand his answer to the question.

Monads

According to Leibniz, reality consists solely of an infinity of extensionless monads and their mental states. Reality consists of substances, which must be simple. For this reason he calls them 'monads' (from the Greek word 'monas', meaning 'unity' or 'that which is one'). On the 30th April 1687, Leibniz writes to Arnauld:

> what is not truly *one* being is not truly one *being*.

The claim that substances must be simple has two implications: first, it means that material objects are not real, and second, it implies that monads are like minds and lack spatial extension. Reality merely appears to consist of spatial physical objects. To illustrate this point, Leibniz uses the analogy of a rainbow. In a rainbow, colorless particles of water are seen as colored. Similarly, an aggregate of individual unextended substances are perceived as extended. Reality is so perceived by the monads themselves. In this way, physical spatial bodies are merely the appearances of and for mind–like monads.

As we have seen, the basis of these conclusions is the assertion that substances must be simple. This assertion itself follows from seemingly innocuous premises. First, any compound (that is, anything which has parts) is ultimately only a collection of simples (that is, things without parts). In other words, compounds require simples. They would not exist but for the simples upon which they depend. However, substances, by the very definition of the term, do not depend on anything else, and therefore substances cannot be compounds. Consequently, they must be simples, without parts. We can summarize Leibniz's argument in two parts as follows:

Part I:

1. A compound is nothing but a collection of simples
2. <u>Anything with parts depends for its reality on those parts.</u>
3. Therefore, any compound depends for its reality on simples

Part II:

3. Any compound depends for its reality on simples
4. <u>Substances do not depend for their reality on anything else</u>
5. Therefore, anything with parts cannot be a substance

Note that the conclusion of the first part serves as a premise in the second part. The overall conclusion of the whole two part argument is that all substances must be simple. From this conclusion, it follows that matter cannot be a substance and that substances must be non–spatial monads.

Monads and Causality

In his *Monadology*, Leibniz says that "each substance is like a world apart, independent of everything but God." He means that no created substance can interact with any other created substance. Leibniz characterizes monads as "windowless" because they can neither receive nor impart any causal influence. Substances cannot interact because the proposition 'A acts on B' is relational and reduces to a simple subject–predicate proposition about the properties of A and B respectively. Furthermore, the interaction between substances is impossible because each substance has its own complete concept which predetermines all its predicates at all times. Each individual substance has a predetermined and self–contained history that unfolds with the necessity of a mathematical series in accordance with its own individual nature and without any outside influence, except that of God.

Leibniz argues that there must be an infinity of substances. Because of the principle that God wills the best of all possible worlds, there must be as much variety in the world as is possible and, therefore, God has created an infinite number of monads. This is an important point because it connects Leibniz's two definitions of contingency. He defines a contingent proposition as one which is true in virtue of the principle of the best, and he also defines a contingent truth as one that requires an infinitely long proof. These two definitions are linked because God, in creating the best universe, creates an infinite number of substances but also, because of this, the task of explaining any single contingent fact is infinitely complex.

Monads in the Mirror

Leibniz says that all things are connected: any individual substance stands in relation to all other substances. When we specify the complete concept of Julius Caesar, we must mention his relations to all other substances in the universe. Otherwise, the concept of Julius Caesar would not be complete. In other words, the complete concept of a substance A contains relations to all other things at all times. In this sense, any individual substance expresses the whole universe.

According to Leibniz, this means that, from the predicates of any substance alone, it is possible to infer all the predicates of all other substances. This is why he says "at every moment each monad mirrors the whole universe from its own special point of view." The basis of these claims is that relations are reducible to the properties of substances. As we saw in chapter 4, he argues that the relations between A and B can be inferred from the properties of A alone or from the properties of B alone. Given that all substances stand in relation to each other, this view of relations is equivalent to the claim that each substance expresses the whole universe.

Points of View

Each monad reflects the universe from its own point of view, which is characterized by the relative confusion of its perceptions. Because of the principle of the identity of indiscernibles, no two monads can have the same perceptions. However, in a way, the perceptions of each monad are the same as those of any other monad, because the perception of each monad is simply a reflection of the whole universe, that is of all the monads. Nevertheless, the perceptions of monads differ with respect to their state of confusion. What each monad perceives more or less clearly defines its own unique point of view. For example, at this time I have clear perceptions of a computer screen and only very indistinct perceptions of the other side of the room. The varying clarity of perceptions explains perspective, without having to treat spatial relations as something ultimately real. It explains how monads appear to stand in different spatial relations to each other when reality is non–spatial.

Because the perceptions of monads are to varying degrees confused, there is a hierarchy of monads. There are three kinds of monad: bare monads, animal souls, and rational souls. Bare monads have a completely unconscious perception and have no memory. An infinite aggregate of these monads form the unextended basis of what appears to be extended physical objects. Animal souls have some degree of memory and discrimination of their perceptions. Rational spirits alone have self–consciousness or apperception; they can rationalize and have knowledge of good and evil: these are the souls of humans and angels.

Pre–Established Harmony

The mirroring by each monad of all others underlies the appearance that there is a universal causal interaction between monads. But since there are no such causal relations, this mirroring cannot be explained causally. Each monad develops spontaneously and in isolation, in accordance with its predetermined nature. How, then, can there be correspondence and correlation between the unfolding self-contained history of all the monads? How can a change in any one monad be reflected in the changing state of any other monad, when there is no causality between them? Leibniz rejects the occasionalist view that God constantly intervenes in the course of the world. Instead, he advances the doctrine of pre–established harmony. According to this doctrine, God created each monad and its disposition so that at each instant the perceptions of each and every monad will correspond in every detail. God determines the nature of each monad so that its state will be co–ordinated in a pre–established harmony without the need for interference.

A Contemporary Likeness

There is no doubt that Leibniz's metaphysics strikes most readers as strange. This is why we have explained carefully the arguments that lead to that position.

Very roughly, we can characterize the basics of Leibniz's ontology as follows: the universe consists in an infinity of dimensionless points of active force, each of which reflects and is in harmony with all the others. Put in this way, the view is not as alien as it may first sound. Indeed, it has similarities to some views in contemporary physics; for example,

> It is the point event in space time that is the basic concept (of relativity). In principle all structures have to be understood as forms in a generalized field which is a function of all the space time points (Bohm and Hiley, p. 352)

and

> In the implicate order the totality of existence is enfolded within each region of space and time. So whatever part, element, or aspect we may abstract in thought, this still enfolds the whole (Bohm, p.172)

I am not claiming that Leibniz anticipates contemporary physics. The point is rather that we should not dismiss his views merely on the grounds that they are strange.

9
God

The Reconciliation

One of the projects that Leibniz pursued for most of his adult life was the reconciliation of the Catholic and Protestant churches in Germany. In part, his perseverance was based on his understanding that Christianity should be above all charity and love. Leibniz was a Lutheran, but he argued that the two churches should be reconciled because "the true and essential communion, which makes us part of the body of Jesus Christ, is charity." (p.31, Riley).

He was motivated to work seriously on this project first by Boineburg around 1669. They agreed on a basic strategy to promote unification: Lutherans could agree to the conclusions of the Council of Trent apart from a few passages, which could be given a Lutheran interpretation that was not in discord with Catholic teaching. The idea was to obtain from the Pope a statement to effect that these interpretations were not contrary to the Catholic faith. On this basis, Leibniz would then compose a work, *Catholic Demonstrations,* which would show the compatibility of the two churches. These plans were halted by Boineburg's death in 1672.

In 1677, the Catholic Emperor in Vienna sent Bishop Rojas de Spinola to the court of Hanover to enlist the help of Duke John Frederick in a campaign to unite the two churches in Germany. In 1679, Leibniz explained his own ideas for the unification of the two churches to Duke Friedrich, his new patron who was a Catholic. He expounded the original idea and strategy, adding the overly optimistic claim that the proofs would be written in the universal language to make them incontrovertible. He revived the project of the *Catholic Demonstrations*. The Duke was planning to make a trip to Italy and agreed to speak to the Pope, Innocent XI. However, Leibniz was thwarted again; in early 1680, the Duke died while on his voyage.

In 1683, the Turks marched on Vienna. Rojas called a meeting in Hanover of Catholic and Protestant theologians to promote the union of the two churches in the face of the Muslim threat. Probably for this meeting, Leibniz wrote *Theological System,* a statement of Catholic faith that might be acceptable to Protestants. Despite the strong sympathy he expressed for the Catholic faith in this work and in other places, Leibniz remained a Lutheran all his life. In 1687, he was offered the appointment of Curator of the Vatican Library, a post which might have led him to become a cardinal. Leibniz refused the post, saying that the Catholic church had made a mistake condemning Galileo.

In 1690, Leibniz tried to renew his project of the reunion of the churches. He entered into correspondence with Bishop Bossuet again and with the theologian Pellison, and advocated his plan on the grounds that it would avert a war between the Empire and France. Leibniz hoped that Bishop Bossuet would use his influence to convince king Louis XIV to restore peace to Europe. In the end, however, Bossuet dashed the idea to the ground by declaring that the Council of Trent had been right and that Protestants were heretics. Finally, in 1695, Leibniz gave up the plan of uniting the two churches.

Creation

In 1696, Leibniz designed a medal to celebrate the discovery of the metaphysical significance of binary numbers. When he explained his idea of binary numbers to Duke Rudolf August, the Duke suggested that they were an analogy for creation. Leibniz sent the Duke the design for a medal illustrating the analogy, refering to it as the "secret of creation." In the binary system all numbers are expressed in terms of 0 and 1. Following the Duke's suggestion, Leibniz thought that this was a model of creation: everything can be derived from 1, representing unity or God, and from 0, nothingness. Planned for the medal was the inscription: "One is enough for deriving everything from nothing."

Leibniz claims that God is the original simple substance upon which all created substances depend from moment to moment. In other words, creation was not a one time, one off event, but is a continual process.

The separation between God and His creation has an important ethical implication: that the world is imperfect. Leibniz is very aware of the problem of reconciling the existence of all-perfect God with the existence of evil in the world. This is the central theme of the *Theodicy*, 1710, which is the only full scale philosophical book he published during his life-time.

It seems that an all-perfect God would not create a world in which evil, such as unnecessary suffering, exists. Therefore, the existence of evil seems to be a refutation of the existence of a perfect God. Of course, Leibniz rejects such an argument. However, he also rejects those, such as Bayle, who claim that religious belief must be founded on faith alone, because belief in God contradicts reason. Leibniz tries to defend belief without abandoning reason.

To do this, he argues two points. First, the world is necessarily imperfect, because otherwise it would be identical to God who is all-perfect. Consequently, complaining that the world is imperfect is like affirming that it should not exist at all. Second, any way of improving this world would automatically make it worse. In other words, this is the best of all possible worlds.

The Best of Possible Worlds

Of course, such a claim seems false, and Leibniz seeks to defend it, largely by explaining what he means. When he claims that this is the best of all possible worlds, Leibniz has in mind certain objective criteria of goodness. In particular, this is the most harmonious of all possible worlds, which means that the world contains the greatest diversity of phenomena and the simplest laws of nature. Each law allows that a "maximum effect" is "achieved with a minimum outlay."

Remember that the world consists of an infinity of independent monads, synchronized by God to act in harmony. Each individual monad is completely determinate and separate. God chooses which of all possible monads to make actual, and He does so in such a way that they all harmonize perfectly, so that each expresses a point of view on the rest. The harmony of material things depends entirely on the harmony of the monads.

Because of its harmony or order, the world is also the most beautiful of all possible worlds. Beauty arises from the fact that the order is produced with the most simplicity. Furthermore, Leibniz defines pleasure as the perception of harmony, and therefore, this world is the most delightful of all possible worlds, offering the most opportunity or potential for happiness.

Moreover, this world must contain the most happiness, because the potential for happiness will be realized when there are spirits, who can be aware of the harmony of the world and feel joy and love as a consequence. Spirits are the most perfect of all the created monads, and thus God, who necessarily seeks perfection will necessarily create the largest number of such spirits possible. Therefore, this must be the most happy of all possible worlds.

Leibniz's claim that this is the best of all possible worlds was satirized by Voltaire in his novel, *Candide*, published in 1759. Voltaire's main character, Dr. Pangloss, suffers a series of misfortunes, but continues to proclaim that this is the best of all possible worlds, despite his many experiences to the contrary.

However, Leibniz would argue that natural disasters are an inevitable by-product of our living in a universe governed by physical laws. Without such laws, life would be much worse. Any attempt to improve the universe would result in its being made even worse.

Perhaps the best way to think about how Leibniz might have replied to Voltaire is as follows. It is certain that an all-perfect God exists and, necessarily, such a God would only create the best of all possible worlds. In the appendix to the *Theodicy*, Leibniz writes that God

> was bound by his goodness to choose such a world as should contain the greatest possible order, regularity, virtue and happiness (Huggard, p. 431)

Arguments for God

Given that an all-perfect God exists, it seems reasonable to argue that this must be the best of all possible worlds. Leibniz thinks that it is certain that an all-perfect God exists and he gives three proofs of His existence.

The Ontological Argument

The first proof of the existence of God is the ontological argument of which he gives two formulations. The first formulation follows that of Descartes and Anselm, according to which God is defined as a being which contains all perfections. The argument is:

1. By definition, God is an absolutely perfect being
2. Existence is a perfection and

3. Therefore, God must exist.

The second formulation of the ontological argument, which is derived from Spinoza, begins with a definition of a necessary being as one whose essence includes existence. The argument is:

1. A necessary being is one whose essence includes existence
2. God is such a being

3. Therefore, God exists

However, Leibniz claims that these arguments are radically incomplete without a proof that God is indeed possible. Without such a supplement, the two versions of the argument effectively only show that if God is possible then He exists.

This defect can be rectified by showing that the concept of God does not contain a contradiction, i.e., that it does not contain incompatible predicates. Leibniz argues this point as follows: God is a being whose essence involves all perfections and, by definition, perfections are always simple unanalysable qualities. He then argues that there cannot be a contradiction in attributing to the same thing any conjunction of simple qualities. Such qualities must be compatible because of the very fact that they are simple. Such qualities are not self-evidently incompatible. Thus, if they were incompatible, this incompatibility would have to be demonstrable. However, there cannot be any demonstrable incompatibility between simple unanalysable qualities, because demonstrating incompatibility requires analysis. Consequently, the idea of God is not self-contradictory.

Cosmological Argument

Unlike the ontological argument, which is a priori and based solely on the nature of the concept of God, the cosmological argument is a posteriori, and is based on the existence of contingent things. There must be a sufficient reason for every contingent fact and event. Even if each event can be adequately explained by previous events, and so on ad infinitum, there still remains how to explain the series of events as a whole. We still require an answer to the questions, 'Why does the series as a whole exist at all?' and 'Why does it proceed as it does?' These questions must have answers because of the Principle of Sufficient Reason, and these answers must be found outside the series of events as a whole, in the existence of a necessary being. The system of nature as a whole must depend on the existence of God. Because contingent things do exist, there must also exist a necessary being.

It might seem that the cosmological argument depends on the assumption that there was a first event. Since the first event cannot be explained by earlier events, it would require an alternative explanation, arguably in terms of the existence of God. However, Leibniz's version of the cosmological argument does not require the assumption of a first event; it is unaffected even if events stretch infinitely in the past. For, explaining each event by previous events ad infinitum does not give a complete reason for any event, because there will then remain unanswered the questions as to why there is a world at all and why it should be as it is. The point is crucial and contentious. If each single event in an infinite series of events can be explained by prior events, does there remain a question about explaining the series as a whole? Leibniz argues that there does.

The cosmological argument contends that, because contingent things exist, there is also a necessary existent. However, this does not show that the necessary existent is God. The first step to do this is to prove that there is only one necessary being. This is proved as follows: because all contingent things are connected, a complete reason for any single one of them is enough for all of them. In effect, Leibniz tries to show that the existence of only one necessary being is a sufficient explanation of nature as a whole.

This single necessary being is indeed God, because the necessary being is a voluntary agent, who chose to create the world by making actual one of the possible worlds. The contingency of the actual world shows that the world was freely chosen, since God's choice could have been different without contradiction.

However, this position faces a difficult question: could God really have chosen a possible world other than this one? The difficulty is that God must have all perfections, and this seems to imply that God must choose the best of all possible worlds. If God could choose otherwise, then He would be less than absolutely perfect. On the other hand, if God could not have chosen otherwise, then His choice was not free. Leibniz's answer to this point is to say that motives for action "incline without necessitating." It is necessary that God should choose as He does, but that God does not choose necessarily. This answer is important, because the source of contingency in Leibniz's metaphysics is the choice of God. If God's choice of which possible world to make actual were not a free choice, then Leibniz's system would be completely deterministic.

Contingency and Existence

Leibniz's metaphysics does contain an account of the contingency of the world. As we saw in chapter 4, he claims that all existential propositions, such as 'Caesar exists', are contingent. The one exception is the statement 'God exists', which is a necessary truth and this is why God is a necessary being. Furthermore, only existential propositions are contingent.

To see why this is so, remember that Leibniz claims that truths such as 'Caesar crossed the Rubicorn' are not contingent, because they do not presuppose that Caesar actually exists. They lack existential import; they merely fix the content of the concept 'Caesar', and are true whether the man exists or not. Thus, non-existential truths, such as 'Caesar crossed the Rubicorn', are different from existential truths, such as 'Caesar exists'. Only existential truths are contingent in Leibniz's system.

Their contingency consists in the fact that the a priori proof of a contingent existential propositions is infinitely long, and involves a reference to the free-will of God. The proof would be infinitely long, because it requires showing that the existential truth is part of a description of the best of all possible worlds, and because there are infinite possible worlds.

However, there is another problem. In Chapter 4 we saw that Leibniz claims that all propositions are reducible to the subject-predicate form, and that their truth consists in the subject-concept containing the predicate-concept. However, this theory of truth apparently does not apply to existential propositions, such as 'Caesar exists'. If it did, then all existential truths would be necessary truths. If the statement 'Caesar exists' were true because the concept 'Caesar' contained the idea of existence, then the statement would be analytic, and Caesar would be a necessary being like God. Consequently, it seems that Leibniz's theory of truth cannot apply to contingent existential propositions. Leibniz was aware of this problem, and tries to overcome it by claiming that to affirm that something contingent exists is to assert that it belongs to or is part of the best of all possible worlds.

The Argument from Pre-Established Harmony

Finally, let us briefly turn to Leibniz's third argument for the existence of God. Monads appear to be in universal interaction but, in fact, they are causally independent of each other. Consequently, the appearance of universal interaction has to be accounted for in terms of a pre-established harmony. This pre-established harmony between an infinity of monads requires the existence of God, who can contemplate and co-ordinate an infinity of states. In other words, there must be a sufficient reason for the pre-established harmony of all monads, and given the infinite nature of this harmony, the only possible reason for such harmony must be God.

In fact, this argument for God is a version of the argument from design according to which a certain feature of the universe, for instance its orderliness, can only be accounted for as the work of God.

10
Ethics

How can we reconcile self-interest as a motivation with the claims of morality, when the latter requires us to love our fellow humans? Leibniz is a psychological egoist. This means that humans are only motivated by self-interest. In particular, he thinks that a person's will is motivated only by the judgment that something is good and to judge that something is good is to think that it contributes to one's pleasure more than one's pain. In the work *Mantissa Codicus iuris Gentium Diplomaticus* (1700), he says that it is in our nature to be impelled only by our own good. Yet, at the same time, Leibniz has a rich and elevated conception of morality, which apparently conflicts with this psychological theory. Leibniz has an interesting way out of this dilemma. However, first, we should examine Leibniz's many faceted conception of morality, including the misconceptions that he tries to eliminate.

Against Misconceptions

Moral rightness should be defined in terms of the natural law. This requires distinguishing the natural law from the laws of society, which can be unjust. Also, this means that our moral obligations do not depend on God.

In the *Common Concept of Justice*, (1702) Leibniz repudiates the position of the English philosopher Thomas Hobbes (1588-1679) who claimed that God has the right to do everything because He is all powerful. For Hobbes, God's will defines what is right and lawful just because God is all powerful. According to Leibniz, this view fails to distinguish right and might:

> This is a failure to distinguish between right and fact. For what one can do is one thing, what one should do, another (Riley, p47).

Justice cannot be what pleases the most powerful. Such a view would be tantamount to changing the meaning of the word 'justice'. Rather than being founded on power, the notions of justice and right are based on goodness and wisdom, as we shall see.

According to Leibniz, "the truths of morality impose upon humans certain duties" and would do so even if God did not exist:

> Even if there were no God, we should nevertheless be obliged to conform to natural law (Theodicy, § 183).

However, this does not mean that Leibniz thinks of God as irrelevant to morality. Far from it for, because God is an exemplar of perfect morality from which we must learn.

The Need for a Positive Notion of Justice

Leibniz repudiates a purely negative view of morality. He defines 'justice' as "a constant will to act in such a way that no-one has a reason to complain of us" (Riley, p.53). As he recognizes, this definition requires an explanation of what counts as a reason for complaint. However, the main point is that it follows from this definition that justice is a positive notion. In other words, we are required not only to refrain from harming others, but also, more positively, to be charitable and to do good by helping others.

Leibniz argues for this conclusion in three steps, starting from the following assumption: if a person harms other people and yet expects them not harm him or her, then those other people have a reason to complain against him or her. Consequently, the person's actions would be unjust. The first step is that the same point applies to preventing harm occurring to others. When one can prevent harm without significant cost to oneself, one should do so. Otherwise, the other person would have reason to complain. The second step is that, given this, the same reasoning also applies to helping others by removing obstacles to their obtaining some good. Given this, the third step points out that the same reasoning applies to positive acts which promote the good of others. Otherwise, the other person could complain: "You easily could have made me happy and you did not do it. I complain; you would complain in the same situation, thus I complain with justice."

From this argument by degrees, Leibniz concludes that justice in particular, and morality in general, do not consist of merely refraining from doing evil or causing harm. They necessitate that we perform good actions and bring benefit to others. Also, he concludes that the rule of reason requires us to put ourselves in the place of others, for this is "the true point of view for judging what is just or not." (p.56, Riley).

Three Levels

In the Preface to the *Codex Juris Gentium Diplomaticus*, 1693, Leibniz explains that there are three levels to morality or justice (Loemker, p.421). The first he calls strict law. At this level, we can assume that people are selfish; consequently, at this level, morality requires the use of external force to prevent people from harming each other. The basis of this legal morality is that no member of the state should be injured by another.

The second level is called equity or charity in the narrow sense. At this level, each person should receive his or her due according to the principles of distributive and retributive justice, and morality requires us to do good to all people in accordance with their due. The basis of this social morality is the respect of other persons.

Leibniz calls the third level of morality, piety. At this level, morality requires us to live honourably. This includes duties that are not covered by the first two levels, such as the duty to respect oneself and not to abuse one's own property. At this third level, morality is based on the fact that "we owe ourselves and our all to God." This morality extends beyond our mortal life and, for this reason, at this level, justice is based on the universal harmony, which consists in the fact that God rules over a community of immortal souls.

The Unity of the Three Levels

Leibniz often defines justice as the charity of the wise. Justice is goodness made to conform to wisdom. Wisdom is an important concept for Leibniz; for example, he defines virtue as the habit of acting according to wisdom. The importance of wisdom is based on the idea that the morality of our actions depends on our understanding. The more we understand the nature of the universe, the more we will be moral.

This assumption about wisdom can be explained in terms of understanding charity or goodness, the other half of the definition of justice. He defines goodness in terms of serving the perfection of intelligent substances. For example, by helping someone, I enhance that person's perfection or qualities of excellence, such as his or her feelings of joy or contentment, or natural capacities.

Perfection has an objective and a subjective side. The subjective side is the feeling of pleasure that the perception of a perfection causes in us. Leibniz defines pleasure as

> the feeling of a perfection or of an excellence, whether in ourselves or in something else (p425, Loemker).

However, sometimes the perfections of other people sometimes displease us. Leibniz argues that they do so not as perfections per se, but because of the circumstances (for example, the beauty of a rival). He also notes that we sometimes feel the pleasure of the perfection of something without understanding what we perceive; this phenomena is the feeling of sympathy.

Perfection also has an objective aspect, namely that it is grounded in harmony and order. In turn this gives rise to beauty and a feeling of love (p.426, Loemker).

Now we can understand the moral importance of wisdom and why, for example, Leibniz defines justice as the charity of the wise. Wisdom is the quality of being able to understand the qualities of excellence and their objective basis in harmony and order.

The three levels of morality correspond to three kinds of pleasure. At the first level, people are assumed to find pleasure only in themselves or their own states and perfections. Assuming that each person is not concerned about other people, morality has to prevent that we harm each other. In contrast, at the second level, we find pleasure in the pleasure of others. In other words, we love others and, at this level, morality enjoins us to be charitable, and to promote the welfare and perfection of other people. Finally, at the third level, we find pleasure in the happiness of God; we love God and morality requires from us universal justice.

Loving God

The third is the highest level of morality. In 1678, Leibniz wrote four dialogues on religion in which he considers the fact that "God has commanded us to love Him above all things." (p.423, ed. Jolley). According to Leibniz, "to love is to find pleasure in the perfection of another." This means that, by knowing God's perfections, we love God and, since He is all perfect, the pleasure we will feel by loving Him will be "the greatest and most durable which can exist." Love of the divine excels all other kinds of love because

> God can be loved with the happiest result since nothing is happier than God, and at the same time, nothing can be conceived more beautiful and more worthy of happiness. (Loemker, p.422)

The Problem and its Solution

The problem is that Leibniz holds a form of egoistic hedonism. In other words, we only act for the sake of our own self-interest (egoism), which consists in pleasurable experience (hedonism). Yet, his moral theory seems to require precisely the opposite: that we care for the interests of others and love God. For example, justice requires that we love other people without seeking their good merely as a means to our own pleasure.

What is the motive required for one to be virtuous or moral? Leibniz believes that the same moral rules apply to both God and human beings. In other words, divine and human justice are comparable, except that God is perfect. This means that we can learn about morality and the motives that it requires by considering God. God is not motivated by fear and hope (of punishment and reward); instead He takes pleasure in, and is motivated by, perfection.

How does Leibniz reconcile these claims with his egoistic hedonism? His answer has three parts. The first part is an analysis of what love is. If we love something, then we take immediate pleasure in its perfection. Therefore, when we love something for its own sake, we take pleasure in it immediately, and not for the sake of something else. It is:

> desired for itself, as constituting (at least) in part the end of our wishes, and as something which enters into our own felicity (p.425, ed. Jolley).

Leibniz admits the possibility of a pure and disinterested love that is "independent of hope, of fear and of regard for any question of utility" (p426, ed. Jolley). However, such a love is not contrary to egoism because it requires that we make the other person's interests part of our interests. "To love or to cherish is to find pleasure in the happiness of another or to accept the happiness of another as one's own (p421, Loemker). In summary, justice requires benevolence, which in turn requires making the perfection of another person a part of one's own happiness.

The second part of the answer is the claim that the greatest happiness a person can feel is loving God, because God is the happiest of all beings. And, since, to love God, it is necessary to love all human beings, the person who loves God will be a just person.

The third part of Leibniz's solution is that the existence of an all-perfect God means that wrong-doing will be punished and that virtuous actions will be rewarded. Despite this, Leibniz thinks that a person who tries to be just merely for the sake of the after-life will never become just. Acting in accordance with the principles of justice merely from the fear of avoiding punishment does not make a person just. He says: "He who obeys God from fear is not a friend of God." The after-life is not the motivating reason for being moral or just, but it is the only way to demonstrate that morality and self-interest coincide.

> In order to really establish by a universal demonstration that everything honorable is beneficial and everything base is harmful, we must assume the immortality of the soul and God (Loemker, p.423).

11
Politics

Leibniz was active in politics both as a diplomat and as the advisor of European nobility. However, his primary concern was the welfare of people. He advanced many ideas to improve the lives of the public, such as better drainage systems and improvements to the educational and health systems. For example, he encouraged the publication of medical statistics in Germany and France. In 1691, when he learned of a new cure for dysentery used in France, he pushed to have the cure introduced in Germany. He advocated preventative medicine and the establishment of a permanent Council of Health to reduce the dangerous epidemics among the poor. He promoted the idea of economic councils and surveys to improve manufacturing and agriculture on the grounds that it is "much better to prevent poverty and misery, which is the mother of all crimes, than to relieve it after it is born" (p.26, Riley). To Duke Friedrich in 1679, he recommended the setting up of a bureau of information and a department store. In 1681, he also made many suggestions to improve the conditions of soldiers and to advance war strategies that would result in fewer casualties. Even his more theoretical ideas, such as the universal calculus, Leibniz thought would be beneficial to humanity in the long term.

This emphasis on public welfare is the cornerstone of his political theory. He claims that justice is that:

> which is useful to the community, and the public good is the
> supreme law - a community, however, not of a few, not of a
> particular nation, but of all of those who are part of the City
> of God and...of the state of the universe (p.30, Riley)

This is very different from the type of theory advanced by, for instance, Locke, which tries to justify the state as a legal authority to protect natural rights, formed through a social contract. In contrast, Leibniz argues that the legitimacy of the state does not depend on any social contract between the participants. It does not depend on its origins at all. What justifies the formation of the state is that it promotes the common good.

Consequently, Leibniz does not claim that the state requires the participation of all the members of society, as does Locke. Writing about Locke's *Two Treatises of Government,* in a letter to Burnett (c1700), he claims that if several men found themselves in a single ship on the open sea, "it would not be in the least conformable either to reason or nature that those who understand nothing of sea-going claim to be pilots" (p.23, Riley). Following the analogy, natural reason dictates that government belongs to the wisest. It would be unjust if it did not.

> "The end of monarchy is to make a hero of eminent wisdom and virtue reign. The end of aristocracy is to give the government to the most wise and most expert. The end of democracy is to make the people themselves agree to what is good for them" (p. 23, Riley)

Leibniz opposes the Lockean idea that all people are born with equal natural rights. Such equality would be certain only if people had the same natural advantages, which clearly they do not. He also rejects Hobbes' view of the social contract according to which in the state of nature, prior to the social contract, there was no moral law. He writes in *Remarks on Shaftesbury's Characteristics* that Shaftesbury successfully refutes those who claim that there is no obligation at all in the state of nature and outside of government.

Furthermore, in the *New Essays,* Leibniz rejects the need for a social contract to explain the origins of civil society. People unite to obtain common ends naturally "as birds flock together to travel in company." In summary, the artificial idea of a social contract is not necessary to explain the origin of Government, nor to justify its legitimacy, nor to explain morality.

However, Leibniz was against arbitrary power, whether of a monarch or of the multitude. He rejected Hobbes' failure to distinguish between power and reason. The political ideal is a union of both. Power is necessary for turning right into fact. Benevolence is necessary for making leaders who will do what is right. The wise and virtuous ought to rule, and they ought to promote improvement in the living conditions, knowledge and virtue of the citizens. "The end of politics after virtue is abundance", so that people "will be in a better position to work in common concert" for those things that "cause the sovereign Author to be admired and loved."

Some aspects of Leibniz's political theory may seem elitist and paternalistic today. However, it is a logical consequence of his hedonistic ethics that he should lay stress on welfare in his politics even at the expense of more standard democratic values. Moreover, it should not be thought that Leibniz was pandering to his patrons. In several writings, he chastises princes and kings for failure to do their utmost to promote the well-being of their subjects. He was well aware that the decisions of a king in a bad mood might cause many deaths.

The Sovereignty of the State

As well as advancing projects for the benefit of the community, Leibniz was political advisor to the House of Hanover and a European diplomat. He was a contemporary of the French king, Louis XIV, who had expansionist aims and was feared by other European countries. Leibniz wrote polemical and satirical tracts against the king, even though he greatly admired the intellectual culture of Paris.

He strove to help the house of Hanover gain the English throne. Leibniz's friend, the Electress Sophie, was the Protestant grand-daughter of the deceased British King James I (1566-1625). Leibniz advised the family how to secure the throne diplomatically by arguing that the British would not want to see the return of the Catholic Stuart family. Leibniz was a subtle, tactful, clever and insistent diplomat.

In 1678, there was a peace conference in Nijmegen to end the conflict between France and the Netherlands. Leibniz, under the pseudonym Caesarinus Fürstenerius, produced a political document for the congress, which was published in 1677. The paper addresses the question of whether the German Electors and Princes should be considered as foreign powers. During Leibniz's time, Germany as a state did not exist. It consisted of many principalities, each with each its own ruler or minor prince. However, each principality was part of the overall Empire, called the Holy Roman Empire, headed by a Hapsburg (Leopold I) and which included Austria, Bohemia, Hungary and Germany. The Emperor was chosen by seven German princes, called Electors. A question that had to answered during the conference was whether these principalities should be considered as states.

Leibniz argues that the principalities should be considered as separate sovereign states. He does so by giving a purely descriptive account of sovereignty, one which does not try to justify the concept by appeal to some law. Leibniz claims that sovereignty is simply being "master of a territory", or having enough power to maintain this mastery. His description fits the situation of the principalities of Germany of the time, which had armies and many of the signs of sovereignty, but still owed allegiance to the Emperor.

Leibniz also supports his analysis by arguing against the idea of absolute sovereignty. An advocate of absolute sovereignty would claim that the principalities of Germany would not qualify as separate sovereign states, because they owe allegiance to the Emperor and are part of the Empire. Consequently, Leibniz tries to undermine the idea of absolute sovereignty. He does so in two ways. First, he argues that the state is not an entity. It is a mere aggregation or collection, like a herd or a gathering. Only individuals are real entities (as we have seen in earlier chapters). Secondly, he takes issue with the claims of Hobbes.

The English philosopher Thomas Hobbes argues in favor of absolute sovereignty. He claims that, without an absolute sovereign, people would be at war with one another, because each has a natural right to all things. According to Hobbes, the only way to avoid such wars is for the people to transfer their rights to the government or king. Hobbes argues that there can only be one government, and it must be centralized in one absolute monarch, because if power were divided among several groups or individual persons, then there would be disagreement among them and war would ensue.

Leibniz rejects these claims. According to Leibniz, apart from the objections mentioned earlier, Hobbes' view is based on a false dichotomy: the only alternative to an anarchical state of nature is an absolute monarch. Leibniz says that this dichotomy does not accord with the experience of Europe, where there is neither of these two situations. Furthermore, Leibniz contends that if there were to be an absolute sovereign, then it would have to be God, "whom alone one can trust in all things."

Hobbes' analysis of the law also supports his idea of absolute monarchy. Hobbes claims that the law is no more than a command. The laws are the commands of a sovereign ruler, and this law should be obeyed because it is commanded. Leibniz rejects this analysis arguing that the content of the law is what matters, namely the promotion of welfare and justice.

International Relations

In the 1670s, Leibniz believed in the idea of a European Christian union. He promoted this idea to unify Europe, and to bring religious schisms and fighting to an end. The idea requires an Emperor to protect Christendom and the Church "against the infidels" (i.e. the Turks). He advocated a ecumenical council that would be the general senate of Christendom. Within this European Christian union, particular states or principalities would continue, but as part of an overarching Christian State. Later in life, Leibniz was less optimistic about the possibility of religious and political unity, and he advocated reliance on international laws and treaties to secure international peace.

12
Concerning Locke

In 1690, Locke published the first edition of the *Essay Concerning Human Understanding*. Five years after the publication of Locke's *Essay,* Leibniz had read several parts of it and had made some comments, which were passed on to Locke. Leibniz's knowledge of the English language was limited, and this must have made his reading of Locke's work difficult. In 1700, Locke's *Essay* was published in French, and Leibniz started to study it in earnest in mid 1703. Around this time, he began to write an extensive commentary on the work, which became *New Essays Concerning Human Understanding.* The first draft of Leibniz's *New Essays* was finished in May 1704. He revised the work and had it ready for publication by November 1704. At the end of the month, Leibniz received the news that Locke had died, and he decided to not publish his work, pointing out that Locke could no longer reply to his comments. He also expressed the concern that he might become embroiled in another controversy.

During the year 1704, Leibniz was in correspondence with Lady Masham, with whom Locke lodged during the years before his death. At this time, Locke himself was too ill to write to Leibniz. After Locke's death in October 1704, Leibniz continued his correspondence with Lady Masham, comparing his own philosophy with that of her father, Cudworth, and commenting on her own work on divine love.

The New Essays

In his book, Locke argues against innate ideas, and tries to show how all our ideas can be derived from sensory experience. In the course of this work, he analyses many important philosophical concepts, such as substance, cause, mind and God, with the primary aim of showing how these concepts must be understood given their empiricist origin - which is to say, on the whole, with a scepticism towards metaphysics.

Leibniz's commentary on Locke takes the form of a dialogue between Philalèthe (lover of truth), representing Locke, and Théophile (lover of God), standing for Leibniz. Leibniz takes issue with the very starting point of Locke's project: the rejection of innate ideas. Leibniz claims that there are necessary truths in metaphysics, ethics, logic, and mathematics that are true, independent of sense experience, and thus can only be known innately, or through a proof that is itself based on innate principles. For instance, the principle of non-contradiction (that a contradiction cannot be true) is innate. So is the principle of sufficient reason, which states that nothing happens without a reason why it is so and not otherwise. These two principles can be known a priori, without appeal to sense-experience, and are the basis of metaphysics.

Leibniz also argues that the recognition of innate ideas is already inherent in Locke's own position. Locke claims that our ideas have two sources in experience: sensation and reflection. Leibniz argues that reflection must be directed towards the mind itself and it is through reflection that we recognize the innate ideas or features of the mind, which are required for the mind to be what it is. These include substance, unity, change, duration, action and perception. Leibniz says:

> Nothing is in the understanding which was not previously in the senses, except understanding itself (Jolley, p.12)

Leibniz also notes that Locke accepts the idea of innate capacities and dispositions and, consequently, the difference between the views of the two thinkers is not so great.

Unconscious Perceptions

One important difference between the two philosophers is that Locke assumes that we must be conscious of our own ideas. Because of this, Locke claims that the notion of innate ideas is absurd; such a notion implies that we have some ideas of which we are not conscious. However, Leibniz takes issue with Locke on his initial premise: that we are conscious of all our ideas. He has two ingenious arguments to show that there must be unconscious ideas. First, in deep sleep, we can be woken by a noise. Consequently, the noise impinges on our mind before we are even conscious of it. Second, if the majority of our ideas were not unconscious, we could not attend to those that are important. Our awareness would be crowded out.

Leibniz claims that all our conscious ideas are composed of minute unconscious perceptions. This is a consequence of the principle of continuity according to which nature never makes leaps. A rope can be torn with great effort only because it is stretched a little by a small force. Similarly, a light can be seen only because of a multitude of perceptions of which we are not aware.

This point illustrates the truth and the importance of the Principle of the Identity of Indiscernibles. Even if two substances or monads appear very much alike, they will differ in their minute, unconscious perceptions.

The Principle of the Identity of Indiscernibles shows problems with various other aspects of Locke's philosophy. For example, Locke apparently argues for the notion of substance in general, understood as a pure substratum in which qualities or properties inhere (see below). According to Leibniz, such a concept makes no sense because there would no way to identity different substances so understood. In other words, the idea is a violation of the Principle of the Identity of Indiscernibles.

Furthermore, Locke's claim that the mind is a blank slate at birth also contravenes the Principle. Minds without ideas have no individuating characteristics. Therefore, the Principle of the Identity of Indiscernibles implies that the mind cannot be blank at birth, and that there must be innate ideas.

Leibniz has a similar argument against the existence of indistinguishable atoms: if they are indistinguishable, then they cannot be distinct. Furthermore, if one were to reply to Leibniz by claiming that such atoms can be distinguished by their spatio-temporal position, then he would counter that the very same point applies to space and time itself. The Newtonian notion of absolute space and time does not make sense, because, among other reasons, it requires the idea of something that has indistinguishable parts.

Metaphysics and Theology

The debate regarding innate ideas has a deep metaphysical and theological significance for Leibniz. According to him, in denying innate ideas, Locke has rejected the basis of a proper understanding of religion. For instance, Locke's empiricist claim that all ideas are derived from experience makes the concept of infinity essentially problematic. Locke uses his theory of concept acquisition to argue that we do not have a positive conception of infinity. We only have the negative idea of a unit repeated without limit i.e. the concept of a potentially infinite quantity.

This means that we cannot meaningfully talk about God's wisdom, power and goodness being infinite, for in such assertions the concept of infinity is being used positively and non-quantitatively. In contrast, Leibniz argues that such assertions can be meaningful, because the idea of infinity is not limited to what can be derived from a finite experience, since the idea of the infinite is innate. For reasons such as these, Leibniz complains that Locke's metaphysics is mean or ungenerous. He writes that Locke "enfeebles the generous philosophy of the Platonists." (Jolley, p.16)

The Soul

In a letter of 1704, Leibniz wrote about the *New Essays*:

> I am above all concerned to vindicate the immateriality of the soul which Mr. Locke leaves doubtful (Jolley, p.102)

In his *Essay Concerning Human Understanding,* Locke argues that there are no grounds for denying that matter might think. According to Locke, we can have no evidence against materialism. Locke argues for this radical claim in two ways. First, he thinks that the notion of substance in general is that of something unknowable. This would apply just as much to the idea of a non-material substance, as it does to material substance. If there were a non-material mind, it would be unknowable. Second, Locke rejects the idea that our personal identity consists in the identity of a non-material substance. In other words, he rejects the claim that personal identity requires the existence of a non-material mind or soul.

Leibniz wholeheartedly rejects Locke's agnostic position regarding materialism. He argues that such a view leaves the immortality of the soul in doubt. The claim that the soul is immortal requires the assertion that it is not material. Let us examine how Leibniz objects to Locke's arguments.

Substance

One of the reasons for Locke's agnosticism concerning the debate about materialism is his view of substance. At least according to one interpretation, Locke claims that the notion of substance is the idea of an unknown substratum that supports properties. Locke criticizes this notion as empty and calls this notion the idea of "something I know not what." This view of substance supports Locke's refusal to reject materialism. If substance is essentially unknowable, then we cannot have grounds for affirming that material substance cannot be conscious.

Leibniz argues against Locke's explanation of the concept of substance claiming:

> if you distinguish two things in a substance, the attributes and their subject, it is no wonder that you cannot conceive anything special in the subject (Remnant and Bennett, p218).

In other words, Locke's explanation of substance illegitimately contrasts a substance with all of its properties and, on this basis, complains that the notion is empty. In contrast, Leibniz rejects the idea of pure substratum as a legitimate way to understand the concept of substance.

As we saw earlier, Leibniz argues that Locke's notion of substratum contravenes the Principle of the Identity of Indiscernibles. Locke's theory implies that there could be two indiscernible substances, which is impossible. Furthermore, Leibniz has his own positive theory of substance, which we have already examined.

Personal Identity

Locke denies that personal identity and immortality require the continued existence of a non-material substance. He claims that the idea of the continued existence of a person through time does not require the existence of a substance, whether material or not. It does not depend on the identity of soul substances, even if there are such things. Instead, personal identity depends on memory. Suppose that the soul of Socrates were reincarnated in the body of the present Mayor of Queenborough. According to Locke, even if this were the case, the Mayor of Queenborough would not be the same person as Socrates, unless the Mayor had Socrates' memories.

In opposition to this position, Leibniz argues that continuity of memory does not constitute, and is not necessary for, personal identity. Rather, it simply counts as usually reliable evidence for the identity of persons. On the contrary, personal identity consists of the identity of a non-material monad, because a person is a non-material being or monad.

In considering these objections to Locke, we should bear in mind Leibniz's own arguments against the traditional notion of matter, and in favor of a non-material view of substance, points which were all dealt with in earlier chapters. For all these reasons, Locke's agnosticism regarding a materialist view of the mind is mistaken.

Essentialism

Locke argues for an anti-essentialist thesis by distinguishing between real and nominal essences. The nominal essence of a substance type or kind, such as gold, is the idea of the observable characteristics that substances of that kind have. For example, we call an object a piece of gold because of its yellow color and its weight. Locke contrasts the nominal essence of gold with its real essence. The real essence is what makes something what it is. For example, in the case of gold, the real essence is the internal constitution or corpuscular structure of the substance. Locke draws this distinction in order to argue that we classify substances according to their nominal essence, and not their real essence. According to Locke, the real essence of substance kinds are unknown to us, and for this reason we make our classifications according to nominal essences only.

In contrast, Leibniz thinks we classify according to real essence, even if it is unknown. He says:

> the name 'gold' signifies not merely what the speaker knows of gold... but also what he does not know (Remnant and Bennett, p. 354).

In other words, even if we do not know the real essence of gold, this does not mean that the word 'gold' only stands for the nominal essence. We can use the word 'gold' to stand for a thing with a real essence that we do not know. Of course, if this were the case, then we would be prone to make mistakes in our classifications. However, such mistakes are quite possible. Indeed, our definitions of the relevant sortal terms (such as 'gold') are always provisional. For instance, the definition of 'gold' might be revised as we learn more about the inner structure of the substance. For example, the definition would change if we found a new test to distinguish counterfeit and real gold (Remnant and Bennett p. 312).

Leibniz sees the importance of this debate for the concept of a human being. According to Locke, what counts as a human being depends on our idea of the nominal essence of the species. In other words, there is an unavoidable arbitrary element in our classification. In contrast, Leibniz claims that the term 'human' refers to a being with a particular real essence, namely that of being rational. Once again, this does not mean that we can always tell whether a creature is human or not. For example, it might be difficult to know whether we should classify a strange looking monster as human. Leibniz also recognizes that external considerations, such as physical shape, are usually used as criteria or signs for identifying a being as human. Nevertheless, the term 'human' refers to a being with a certain real essence.

A final note: we saw in chapter 4 that Leibniz argues that all of the properties of an individual are essential to that individual. This claim is based on the assertion that each individual substance is defined by a complete concept that distinguishes it from all other possible individuals. Leibniz does not discuss this aspect of his theory in his reply to Locke.

13
China

In 1689, when Leibniz was in Rome, he met the Jesuit missionary Claudio Grimaldi, who was President of the Chinese Bureau of mathematics. Leibniz was very interested in the language, technology and philosophy of China. This was an interest he had had since 1660s, and later he became interested in Chinese as a potential example of a universal language.

After this meeting, Leibniz was in regular contact by letter with the Jesuit Mission in China. In 1697, he edited a collection of essays and letters from the mission, entitled *Novissima Sinica* (Latest News from China). A copy of this book came into the possession of Joachim Bouvet, who wrote to Leibniz with more information about China, and a copy of his own work, *A Historical Portrait of the Emperor of China*, which Leibniz included in his second edition of the *Novissima Sinica* in 1699.

In the last year of his life, 1716, Leibniz read two commentaries on some classical Chinese texts (Longobardi and Antoine Sainte-Marie). He was asked his opinion of the books, and in reply he wrote the *Discourse on the Natural Theology of the Chinese,* which we shall discuss later.

Leibniz's work on the philosophy of China is interesting for what it shows about him as a thinker, and for what it reveals about the European attitudes to China of the time. Although Leibniz was one of the most knowledgeable people in Europe concerning Chinese philosophy, he could not read Chinese. He had to rely on the Jesuits in China, such as Bouvet.

Correspondence with Bouvet

The contact with Bouvet is important. The significant correspondence between them consists of 9 letters from 1696-1703 (Leibniz wrote 6 letters to Bouvet after 1703, but never received a reply). In one of his early letters to Bouvet, Leibniz describes the basics of his own philosophy which requires the existence of forces, which the ancient Greeks had called forms, in addition to matter. In reply, Bouvet points out similarities between Leibniz's philosophy and that of the Chinese.

In 1701, Leibniz wrote to Bouvet describing his binary arithmetic, including the analogy with creation (see Ch. 9). Leibniz received Bouvet's enthusiastic reply in 1703, which claims that the secret for understanding the I Ching and the nature of Chinese philosophy lay with Leibniz's binary arithmetic.

Bouvet asserts that the *Book of Changes*, being the oldest Chinese book in existence, represents an ancient culture which had knowledge that was subsequently lost. He says that the lines of the hexagrams of the *Book of Changes* are the very first characters of the Chinese language, and that they represent the principles of an ancient metaphysical system, lost to the Chinese by the time of Confucius (551 BC.). He sent to Leibniz a copy of the Prior to Heaven hexagram, which consists of 64 figures each of six lines, which, according to tradition, was composed 4,500 years ago by Fu Hsi. Bouvet claims that this diagram contains the secrets of the ancient sciences of arithmetic, astronomy, medicine and music. He also claims that the broken lines represent 0 and the unbroken lines, 1, and that the hexagrams represent, among other things, the numbers 0 to 64 in binary form.

Because of this letter, Leibniz had reason to believe that the universal calculus and language he had worked on his whole life had been known to the ancient Chinese. Furthermore, Bouvet had argued that the ancient Chinese had a natural religion, which was in accord with the fundamentals of Christianity. Consequently, Bouvet asserted that the best way to convert the Chinese to Christianity was for the Chinese to relearn the forgotten metaphysics of their past. This too struck a deep chord for Leibniz, who believed that reason can reveal the true religion and that the basic principles of Christianity can be demonstrated clearly using the universal language he was developing.

For these reasons, Bouvet affirmed that Leibniz's universal calculus and binary notation would be useful to the cause of unity in China. In fact, the similarities between the binary numbers and the

83

hexagram depend on where one starts reading the hexagram. In other words, the interpretation is fluid. Furthermore, Bouvet was living in a court of the Manchu rulers, rather isolated from the provinces. The Chinese regarded their Machurian conquerors from the north as foreigners. To counteract this, the Manchurians adopted a very traditional approach to the classics which emphasized the true hidden meaning of works such as the *Book of Changes,* in opposition to the literary Chinese society of the time. In any case, Bouvet thought that the hexagram represented a piece of ancient and long forgotten knowledge, from a time when humans knew more of the universe's secrets.

The Discourse

Leibniz divides the *Discourse on the Natural Theology of the Chinese* into four parts. The first is on God, the second on the notion of spirits and matter; the third on the human soul and immortality, and the fourth on binary numbers and the *Book of Changes.* The first two themes, God and His creation, constitute almost 75% of the total work.

Ricci (1552-1610) spent 28 years in China, during which time he founded the first Catholic mission. He gained the greatest respect among the Chinese literary class for his works written in Chinese. He sought a harmonious approach to his missionary work. Rather than treating Chinese culture as pagan and unworthy of respect and study, Ricci thought that the traditional Chinese metaphysics and customs could be reconciled with Christianity. Therefore, he advocated that the ancient Chinese traditions and rituals should be incorporated into the Christian faith in China.

Longobardi (1565-1655) succeeded Ricci as head of the mission. However, Longobardi took the view that the ancient Chinese culture was materialist, and that the modern culture was atheist. He claimed that Confucianism is incompatible with Christianity. Thus, he advocated that conversion to Christianity requires total renunciation of China's traditions.

Leibniz's main aim in the *Discourse* is to defend the position of Ricci against that of Longobardi. In the first part of the *Discourse,* Leibniz argues that the Chinese do have a concept similar to the Christian idea of God, a claim that Longobardi disputes. The argument hinges on the word 'Li', which Leibniz translates as 'first principle' (§4). Citing Chinese texts, Leibniz calls 'Li', the great and universal cause and argues that there is nothing greater or better than Li. Furthermore, according to the Chinese texts, Li is the source of the five virtues. He concludes that Li has many characteristics which make it comparable to the Christian idea of God.

These points favor Leibniz's position, but Longobardi insists on the accuracy of a materialistic interpretation of the term 'Li', arguing that it should be understood as prime or undifferentiated matter. Leibniz takes issue with this point. First, he accepts that the contemporary Chinese society of his time is largely atheistic, but he claims that ancient Chinese culture reflects a natural religion which is largely compatible with Christianity. Second, classical Chinese philosophy treats Li as an active agent, and not merely passively as prime matter. Third, Leibniz argues that the term 'Li' can also refer to individual souls (or monads) and that this ambiguity is a primary source of Longobardi's confusion.

According to Leibniz, the classical Chinese texts posit a spiritual force that guides events in the universe, and which has various aspects or manifestations, such as Li (first principle), T'ai-chi (ultimate realization), and Tao (the way). Is he right?

Historical background

We know of the views of Confucius (551-479 BC.) mainly from the *Analects,* or the *Lun Yu,* which is a collection of discussions between the master and some of his pupils. Most contemporary commentators on Confucius interpret his thought as agnostic and rationalistic. The *Lun Yu* contains no discussions of metaphysics. Indeed, Confucius shuns abstract metaphysical speculation. The *Lun Yu* is concerned solely with ethics, aesthetics, politics and customs. Its main theme is spiritual self-cultivation through participating in tradition, community and rituals, and through fulfilling the duties associated with one's social roles.

The next great work of Confucian thought is the *Mencius,* written by Mencius (372-289 BC). This work also contains little metaphysical discussion. There is an even later Confucian work, called the *Li Chi,* written and compiled in the second century BC, which contains chapters called the *Great Learning* and *Doctrine of the Mean* that do contain a little metaphysics. Unfortunately, Leibniz thought that these two chapters were written by Confucius.

In the *Discourse,* Leibniz refers to the *Lun Yu, Mencius,* the *Great Learning* and the *Doctrine of the Mean,* as the "Four Books" of classical Confucian thought. However, overall, there is little in these works to substantiate Leibniz's general thesis.

The problem is partly due to Longobardi and Ste. Marie, on whom Leibniz relies for his knowledge of Chinese texts. Both quote at length from a neo-Confucian text, called the *Compendium*, a collection of classical works and commentaries compiled in 1422. However, Longobardi and Ste. Marie do not always distinguish the neo-Confucian commentaries, which often contain metaphysics, from the classical texts, which largely do not.

Leibniz's main interest, however, is in not the classical period of Chinese history following Confucius (from the 6th to the 3rd centuries BC.), but rather in the semi-legendary ancient period many centuries before that. In this, Leibniz was influenced by the views of Bouvet, who thought that the *I Ching* dated from 3,000 BC. Leibniz shared Bouvet's idea that, during its ancient past, China was ruled by sage kings, who were naturally religious.

Probably, Chinese civilization started in 19th century BC., about a thousand years later than Leibniz thought. The oldest parts of the *I Ching*, the hexagrams that fascinated Leibniz so much, probably date from about 1,000 BC. However, the commentaries that discuss the meaning of the hexagrams were probably written in the 3rd century BC. In short, we know virtually nothing about the metaphysical beliefs of the ancient Chinese, contrary to what Leibniz supposed.

Conclusion

Despite these problems, Leibniz's scholarly text on Chinese philosophy is a pioneering work. He wrote at a time when very few philosophers were interested in China. Furthermore, in Leibniz's work, we can see the diplomat in him motivating him to find unity between East and West. Also we can see, in the last months before his death, the optimism and benevolence that pushed him to such great efforts throughout his life.

Bibliography

Adams, Robert Merrihew, *Leibniz: Determinist, Theist, Idealist*, Oxford, 1994

Aiton, E.J., *Leibniz: a Biography*, Adam Hilger, 1985

Bohm, D., *Wholeness and the Implicate Order*, Ark, 1983

Bohm,D. & Hiley B., *The Undivided Universe*, Routledge, 1993

Broad, C.D., *Leibniz: an Introduction*, Cambridge, 1975

Brown, Stuart, *Leibniz*, University of Minnesota, 1984

Durant, *The Age of Louis XIV*, Simon and Schuster, 1963

Frankfurt, H.G., ed., *Leibniz: a Collection of Critical Essays*, Doubleday, 1972

Hooker, M, ed., *Leibniz: Critical and Interpretative Essays*, Minneapolis, 1982

Ishiguro, H., *Leibniz's Philosophy of Logic and Language*, Duckworth, 1972

Kneale, W. and M., *The Development of Logic*, Oxford, 1962

Leibniz, ed. Huggard, E.M., *Theodicy*, Open Court, 1985

Leibniz, ed. Loemaker, L, *Philosophical Papers & Letters*, Reidel, 1969

Leibniz, ed. Martin, R. and Brown, S., *Discourse on Metaphysics and related writings*, Manchester, 1988

Leibniz, ed. Parkinson, G., *Logical Papers*, Clarendon Press, 1966

Leibniz, ed. Parkinson, G., *Philosophical Writings*, Deent, 1973

Leibniz, ed. Remnant,P. and Bennett, J., *New Essays on Human Understanding*, Cambridge, 1981

Leibniz, ed. Riley, P., *Political Writings*, Cambridge, 1988

Leibniz, ed. Rosemont,H., and Cook.D, *Discourse on the Natural Theology of the Chinese*, Hawaii, 1977

Leibniz, *The Leibniz – Arnauld Correspondence*, Manchester University Press, 1967

Mackie, J.M., *Life of Godfrey Liiam Von Leibnitz*, Gould, Kendall and Lincoln, Boston, 1845

Martin, G., *Leibniz: Logic and Metaphysics*, Barnes& Noble, 1967

Mates, Benson, *The Philosophy of Leibniz*, Oxford, 1986

Mungello, D, *Leibniz and Confucianism: the Search for Accord*, University of Hawaii Press, 1977

Jolley,N. (ed.), *The Cambridge Companion to Leibniz*, 1995

Parkinson, G.H.R., *Logic and Reality in Leibniz' Metaphysics*, Garland, 1985

Rescher, Nicholas, *Leibniz: an Introduction to his philosophy*, Blackwell, 1979

Ross, George MacDonald, *Leibniz*, Oxford, 1984

Thomson, Garrett, *Descartes to Kant*, Waveland Press, 1997

Thomson, Garrett, *On Locke*, Wadsworth, 2001